JANE AUSTEN

JANE AUSTEN
by GUY RAWLENCE

DUCKWORTH
3 HENRIETTA STREET
LONDON   W.C.2

HASKELL HOUSE PUBLISHERS Ltd.
Publishers of Scarce Scholarly Books
NEW YORK. N. Y. 10012
1972

HASKELL HOUSE PUBLISHERS Ltd.
Publishers of Scarce Scholarly Books
280 LAFAYETTE STREET
NEW YORK, N. Y. 10012

Library of Congress Cataloging in Publication Data

Rawlence, Guy, 1888–
    Jane Austen.

    (Great lives)
    Reprint of the 1934 ed.
    Bibliography: p.
    1. Austen, Jane, 1775–1817.
PR4036.R3 1972   823'.7 [B]   74-39869
ISBN 0-8383-1405-8

CONTENTS

I wish to acknowledge my indebtedness to Mr. R. A. Austen-Leigh, part author of *Jane Austen : Her Life and Letters*, for permission to make use of certain material in his book. And to Mrs. Sanders, and her publishers (Messrs. Chatto & Windus), for allowing extracts to be taken from *Love and Freindship*.

GUY RAWLENCE

CHRONOLOGY

1775....Birth of Jane Austen at Steventon, Hampshire, 16th December.

1784....Jane and her sister Cassandra (born 1773) at Mrs. Latourelle's School at Reading.

1790–1793. *Love and Freindship* and other Juvenilia written.

1794....Probable date of *Lady Susan*.

1796....*First Impressions* (afterwards entitled *Pride and Prejudice*) begun.

1797....*First Impressions* refused by Cadell, a London publisher.

Sense and Sensibility begun.

1798....First visit to Godmersham, Kent, the property of her brother Edward, who took the name of Knight.

Northanger Abbey begun.

1801....The Austens move to Bath.

1803....*Northanger Abbey* sold, but not published.

1804....Probable date of *The Watsons*.

1805....Death of the Reverend George Austen.

Move to Southampton.

1809....Move to Chawton, near Alton, Hampshire.

1811....*Sense and Sensibility* published.

1812....*Mansfield Park* begun.

1813....*Pride and Prejudice* published.

1814....*Emma* begun.

Mansfield Park published.

1815....*Emma* published.

1816....*Persuasion* finished. It was probably begun in 1815.

1817....*Sanditon* begun.

Goes to Winchester, 24th May.

Death, 18th July.

Burial in Winchester Cathedral, 24th July.

CHAPTER I

1775–1788

For the most part the characters of Jane Austen's novels live in the country. From time to time they visit London or Bath, but chiefly their world is rural – though not bucolic. They pass their lives in rectories and manors, with nicely disposed gardens, the feature of which appears to be a shrubbery, set in a mild, pleasant landscape, usually remarkable for its hedgerows. They are comfortably circumstanced people, many are wealthy, and if there is poverty it is of the most genteel description. There is about everything an air of abundant leisure. The women are tolerably free from household and domestic duties ; the men are so unoccupied that they can pay morning calls, and are always available for picnics, walks, and four o'clock dinners. Children, though numerous, seldom interfere with the lives of their elders. Everyone seems a little self-satisfied.

That is the impression the reader obtains from the novels, and one which he is apt to associate

with their author. It is in some ways a false
impression. One is inclined to think that the only
problems encountered by these people are problems of the heart, and, so insistent are they upon
them, that in other directions they are heartless.
But because different perplexities and problems
of life are not stressed in the novels it is un-
reasonable to conclude that their originator was
ignorant or callous in regard to the inevitable
rubs of life. As we know, to satiation, of the
tragedy which can lie behind the grease-paint
grin of the clown, so we may suspect that an
understanding of disaster, death, and disillu-
sionment can lie behind a quizzing-glass.

Certainly one must admit that Jane was a
woman of limited experience. The world of her
fiction was essentially her world. She never
travelled much more than a hundred miles from
the Hampshire village where she was born ; and
there is no evidence that she wished to do so.
She moved from parsonage to country house, from
lodgings at Bath to lodgings at Lyme, just as her
characters move. She passed her life among the
same kind of people as they were. But though her
field of study was limited, it is unfair to argue
she was limited in emotion. She was a Vermeer
among novelists. And one does not accuse
Vermeer of narrowness or lack of emotional depth

because he restricted himself to painting Dutch interiors and views of his native Delft.

Jane had an exquisite sense of selection and proportion that prompted her to choose for portrayal the surroundings which were hers, and men and women whose like she knew and whose characters she could illuminate with her peculiar intensity of vision. Perhaps, had she ventured, she could have brought this perception to bear upon persons other than frequenters of parlours and assembly rooms, and have come nearer to nature than the wilderness of a private park. But there was a reticence in her character which forbade it, a mistrust of betraying, not only ignorance, but feelings and passions which, possibly, everyone save her beloved sister Cassandra was unaware she possessed. It is conceivable, too, that however often she might indulge in ridicule of others she would have been sensitive of a ridicule which might have been aimed at herself had she blundered when describing persons, scenes, and events drawn from imagination rather than from observation. Therefore she restricted herself to the sort of world which was hers, and the sort of people who were her relations, friends, and acquaintances.

The life of Jane Austen was very much the life of her characters, without the drama and intrigue which are necessary to a novel, and without that heightening of light and shade which is necessary to comedy.

The Austens were a Kentish family, already settled at Horsmonden, near Sevenoaks, in Elizabethan days. Here they prospered in trade, and by the beginning of the eighteenth century they and their relatives were firmly established in the county as people of some wealth and position, and holders of armorial bearings.

George Austen – Jane's father – son of William Austen, a surgeon, was born in 1731. Orphaned at the age of six, he was brought up by his uncle, Francis Austen, a solicitor, of Tonbridge. He was educated at Tonbridge School, whence, with a " Smyth " exhibition, he went to St. John's College, Oxford, where subsequently he became a resident Fellow. In 1758 he was given the appointment of Second Master at Tonbridge School ; but returned to Oxford a few years later. Meanwhile one of his sisters, Philadelphia, went to India and married a certain Dr. Hancock of Calcutta, who was a close friend of Warren Hastings.

In 1760, George took Holy Orders, and in the following year his cousin, Thomas Knight, of Godmersham, not far from Canterbury, presented him with the living of Steventon in Hampshire, where he owned considerable property ; while, soon after, his uncle Francis bought him the adjacent living of Deane – which, however, did not fall vacant until 1773.

It seems that he did not reside, or do duty, at Steventon for three years. A moderate period for those times, when it was by no means an uncommon practice of the clergy to be absentees. Hannah More, writing of Somerset at this date, says : " We have in this neighbourhood thirteen adjoining parishes without so much as even a resident curate." And again : " No clergyman has resided in this parish for forty years."

In 1764, however, on his marriage, he moved to Steventon, where he remained until his retirement in 1801. For, though he appears to have been a man of considerable scholarship and culture, he did not attain any advancement in the Church. Possibly he was without any great ambition and was content in continuing to be the parson of two obscure country villages. For some years he augmented his income by taking resident pupils. One of these, the son of Warren Hastings, was already in his charge before his marriage.

The Reverend George was a man of striking appearance. At Oxford he was known as " the handsome Proctor," and late in life a grand-daughter remarks upon his good looks, particularly mentioning the " milk-whiteness " of his hair. " It was very beautiful," she writes, " with short curls above the ears. His eyes were not large, but of a peculiar and bright hazel. My aunt Jane's were something like them. . . ." In character one has the impression he was amiable, worthy, and estimable, but it was from their mother that Jane, her sister, and brothers inherited the qualities of intelligence, humour, and charm which were common to most of them.

Mrs. Austen before marriage was Cassandra Leigh, daughter of the Reverend Thomas Leigh, a Fellow of All Soul's and holder of the College living at Harpsden in Oxfordshire. Cassandra, who at the time of her marriage was twenty-five, was a " slight woman, with fine, well-cut features. . . . She was amusingly particular about people's noses, having a very aristocratic one herself." She had wit, courage, good humour, and a vigorous constitution, for, though we often read of her illnesses and complaints, she lived to be nearly ninety, and at the age of seventy was an energetic gardener.

The marriage of George and Cassandra took place at Bath. Immediately the ceremony was over, the pair proceeded to Steventon, halting one night at Andover. On this brief honeymoon, Mrs. Austen wore a scarlet riding-habit, which was later to be cut up into suits for her own children, and they were, rather oddly, accompanied by Warren Hastings' son, then a boy of six. It is to be hoped that he took to this brightly clad lady who was to be his foster-mother. At any rate she took to him, for, when the boy died a few years after, she declared " that his death had been as great a grief to her as if he had been a child of her own."

The Rectory to which George Austen brought his bride no longer exists, but from descriptions, and contemporary sketches, one can gain a clear idea of it. The house was built on the slope of a narrow valley, and, like many old houses, faced north, an aspect which was considered to be more healthy than one exposed to enervating sunshine and humid south-westerly winds.

This parsonage was of moderate proportions. It contained three sitting-rooms, seven bedrooms, and two attics in the gable. It was plainly built. Mr. J. E. Austen Leigh, author of the *Memoir of Jane Austen*, published in 1870, says : " The rooms were finished with less elegance than would now be found in the most ordinary dwellings. No cornice marked the junction of wall and ceiling : while the beams which supported the upper floor

BA

projected into the rooms below in all their naked
simplicity, covered only by a coat of paint or
whitewash."

A short drive led to a gravel-sweep outside the
front-door, and on this side the house was closely
set with spruce, elms, and chestnuts. At the back
was a mixed flower and vegetable garden,
surrounded by a cob wall, with a strawberry-
lined grass path, and a sundial. At the top of
this garden, which sloped abruptly, was a turfed
terrace, from which a path, called by the Austens
"The Wood Walk," led pleasantly and um-
brageously along the side of the valley.

How much alteration and improvement was
effected by George Austen it is impossible to tell,
but it is likely that he did a good deal, and as
late as 1800, the year before he left Steventon,
Jane speaks, in a letter, of a new plantation, and
a small orchard of apples, pears, and cherries.
Certainly the Austens lived comfortably – though
with a family of eight, together with pupils and
visiting relatives, with, to our minds, some con-
striction. Two indoor servants were kept, for
several years a carriage and pair, and one may
imagine a way of living, if not opulent, certainly
neither frugal nor parsimonious in this square
house, with its sashed-windows and high-pitched
roof.

About 1825, a new rectory was built, facing the
sun on the opposite side of the valley, and the
modern pilgrim to Jane Austen's birthplace can
see no trace of her home other than a pump,
standing beside what was once the house-well,
and the terrace sloping along the hillside which
was, in Jane's days, "The Wood Walk." It is a
little melancholy.

Both the villages of Steventon and Deane were
small and secluded – a mere scatter of cottages –
set in a gently undulating landscape about a mile
apart. Between them ran the turnpike from
Andover to Basingstoke, along which passed the
mail-coaches twice a day. This road was in
tolerable condition, but elsewhere the roads were
narrow lanes or tracks, and it is recorded that
when, in 1771, Mrs. Austen was moving house
(why it is not easy to say ; possibly, for some
reason, the Austens had been living at Deane for
a time) shortly before the birth of her son, Henry,
the ruts in the lane were so deep that it was
impassable for a carriage, and she made the
journey in a waggon, lying on a feather-bed
placed on the top of pieces of furniture and household goods.

The difficulties of transport, however, did not
deter friends from seeing one another, and there
was a frequent interchange of visits between the

Austens and their neighbours. The nearest of these was a family named Digweed, who rented Steventon Manor from Mr. Knight, George Austen's cousin, and patron of the living. The landlord not being resident on his property, the Austens in some degree represented him, and so added something to their importance in the district. Other friends were the Lefroys at Ashe, the Withers of Manydown Park, and the Harwoods of Deane House – an ancestor of whom is said to have been the model of Fielding's Squire Western. Life, then, for the Austens, though in a backwater, was not without variety, and long before Jane, in later years, visited Bath, London, and elsewhere, she was acquainted with numerous people, and moved freely in the local society of the county. That society whence, with her perception, her insight, and her acute sense of character, she drew the persons of the novels.

Jane was the seventh of a family of eight. She was born on the 16th of December, 1775. On the same day, George wrote to his sister, Philadelphia Hancock, now returned with her daughter, Elizabeth, from India, as follows :

"DEAR SISTER, – You have doubtless been for some time in expectation of hearing from Hampshire, & perhaps wondered a little we

were in our old age grown such bad reckoners,
but so it was, for Cassy certainly expected to
be brought to bed a month ago ; however last
night the time came, & without a great deal of
warning, everything was soon happily over.
We have now another girl, a pleasant plaything
for her sister Cassy, and a future companion.
She is to be Jenny. . . ."

Jane, like her sister – who was two years older
than herself – and her brothers, was put out to
nurse in the village. To us it seems a curious
custom, but in those days it was a common one,
and the Austens, like many other parents, were
content with a daily visit to their children in some
cottage during the first two or three years of their
lives.

At the age of six, Jane, pleading not to be
separated from her already adored sister, Cassandra, was sent with her to a school at Oxford,
kept by a Mrs. Cawley, of whom all that is known
is that she was a " stiff-mannered " person, widow
of a Principal of Brasenose College. After a time
this lady moved her school to Southampton,
where Jane and Cassandra caught what in those
times was called a " putrid-fever " (probably
diphtheria) and were gravely ill. Mrs. Cawley
did not report the matter to the Austens, and it

was the girls' cousin, Jane Cooper, also a pupil at the school, who wrote to Steventon Rectory. Mrs. Austen and Mrs. Cooper immediately set off to Southampton, bearing some non-specified remedy which is said to have saved Jane's life. But unfortunately it appears to have been ineffective with Mrs. Cooper, who caught the infection, from which she died soon after.

Presumably, after this experience, the Austens were dissatisfied with Mrs. Cawley's qualifications as a guardian for their daughters. At any rate the two sisters were taken away from Southampton, and, together with Jane Cooper, sent to the Abbey School at Reading. This establishment was famous in its day, under the charge of Madame Latourelle, an Englishwoman married to a Frenchman, who, however, spoke no word of her husband's tongue. She is described by Mrs. Sherwood, a pupil at the school a few years later, as " a stout person, hardly under seventy, but very active although she had a cork leg. She had never been seen or known to have changed the manner of her dress. Her white muslin handkerchief was always pinned with the same number of pins, her muslin apron always hung in the same form. . . ." The school must have been a pleasant, and even romantic place, with the ruins of the Abbey in its garden, where, as Mrs. Sherwood writes, " the young ladies were allowed to wander under tall trees in hot summer evenings." Moreover, Madame Latourelle and her assistant, Madame St. Quentin, do not appear to have been rigid disciplinarians, for at least on one occasion the three girls were allowed to dine at an inn with their brothers, Edward Austen and Edward Cooper.

It is uncertain when Cassandra and Jane returned home, there to complete their education under the guidance of Mr. Austen. This gentleman's time must have been largely occupied with teaching, for he still took pupils, besides educating his sons, two of whom he prepared for the University. Possibly the sisters had teachers from Basingstoke, for Jane knew some Italian, and enough French to read easily. Though it is likely that she learnt that language mostly from her cousin, Elizabeth, Mrs. Hancock's daughter, who had been educated in Paris, and in 1781 had married the Comte de Feuillade. She came to England when Jane was eleven, and was often at Steventon, particularly during the early years of the French Revolution. Later she was to marry Jane's brother, Henry.

To this time, or a little later, belong the annotations, in Jane's handwriting, of a copy of Oliver Goldsmith's *History of England*. They are amusingly direct and succinct, and indicate the trend of her youthful politics. (In after life she was described as a " moderate Tory.") For instance, beside a passage describing the activities of Cromwell and his followers, she writes : " Oh ! Oh ! The Wretches !" Of the Stuarts : "A family who were always ill-used, BETRAYED OR NEGLECTED, whose virtues are seldom allowed, while their errors are never forgotten." And of the death of Lord Balmerino, executed in the rebellion of '45 : " Dear Balmerino ! I cannot express what I feel for you ! "

Mr. Austen is described by one of his sons as " being not only a profound Scholar, but possessing an exquisite taste in every species of Literature," so it is to be presumed that Jane, as well as other members of her family, was early grounded in English literature. But apparently she was not – when in her teens, at all events – a very great reader, for late in life she deplored to a niece, when criticising a novel which she had written, that in her youth she herself had spent more time in writing than in reading. Later, though she showed a catholic taste both in her choice and judgment of books, she does not appear to have been widely read. Certainly there was nothing of the blue-stocking about her.

For the rest, she drew a little – an accomplishment common among the Austens in an agreeably amateur way – she played tolerably well, and she sang " very sweetly."

She was a notable needlewoman throughout her life. Most of her leisure she was engaged in making garments for the poor, for herself, or doing extremely fine embroidery. There is still in existence an example of this, worked by her, when she was seventeen, for her friend, Mary Lloyd, who was leaving the neighbourhood. It is a housewife, and was presented with these lines :

> *This little bag I hope will prove*
> *To be not vainly made ;*
> *For should you thread and needles want,*
> *It will afford you aid.*
>
> *And as we are about to part,*
> *It will serve another end :*
> *For when you look upon this bag,*
> *You'll recollect your friend.*

The Austens were not wealthy, but the £600 a year which George Austen received from his twin incumbencies, together with the fees for the pupils who came to Steventon Rectory, was a comfortable income for those days. Nevertheless, economy was practised, and it is recorded that

Mrs. Austen " had no taste for expensive show or
finery." But, though simple, life for the Austens
seems to have been easy and agreeable, and one
has the impression that it was a very happy
one.

Of the brothers, to whom Jane was a devoted
sister, following their affairs and well-being with
an ardent interest and sympathy, the eldest,
James, entered the Church early ; Henry did
likewise, but considerably later in life, after
serving a long term in the Militia and being
partner in a banking firm ; Edward inherited a
large property from his uncle, Thomas Knight,
assumed that name, and developed into an excellent specimen of what is called " a country
gentleman " ; Charles and Francis were both in
the Navy, and ended by being admirals. Finally
there was George, of whom nothing is known
beyond the fact that he was an invalid, prone to
fits. Theirs certainly were varied careers, but all
the brothers – with the exception of the unfortunate George – appear to have been endowed
with humour, good looks, good sense, and good
natures.

One imagines Jane in her childhood, sharing, so
far as was possible, the life, the games, and amusements of her brothers, and probably being their
confidante. One can, for instance, picture her

immense excitement when her brother, Francis,
aged eight, and a year older than herself, purchased, for the sum of £1 11s. 6d. a chestnut pony
named Squirrel (abbreviated by his brothers to
the monosyllabic Scug), and she would inevitably
share his pride when, after riding the pony to
hounds for a season or two, he sold it at a profit of
a guinea. She would share something of their
excitements in the hunting-field, and their increasing prowess with a gun or at cricket. She
would be both thrilled and disconsolate when first
Francis, and later Charles, went to the Royal
Naval Academy at Portsmouth. She would share
with them and Cassandra in the enthralling
activities of the theatricals which at one time were
regular features of life at Steventon, taking place
at Midsummer and Christmas, when Mr. Austen's
pupils had their holidays. In summer, the theatre
was a barn, in winter, the drawing-room – which
must have necessitated a very restricted audience.
Among the plays performed were *The Rivals*,
Which is the Man ? and a farce called *Bon Ton*. For
these performances, Jane's eldest brother, James,
wrote the prologues and epilogues. Jane herself
took part at least on one occasion, and probably a
recollection of these performances was in her
mind when, many years later, she described the
disastrously frustrated theatricals at Mansfield

Park, when a choice was made of *Lovers' Vows*, a play the language of which was " so unfit to be expressed by any woman of modesty."

Of Jane's childhood and girlhood there are no anecdotes either of precocity or stupidity, goodness or badness. We have, indeed, few references to her, but there are two made by a cousin, Philadelphia Walter. The one is : " Jane is whimsical and affected." And the other, made a little later : [Jane] " is not at all pretty and very prim, unlike a girl of twelve." They are somewhat contradictory, and from this one may reasonably suppose that Jane was a creature, even in those days, of moods and behaviours which varied with her company. With comparative strangers she was probably " prim," due to a shyness which might well be hidden by what Philadelphia calls affectation ; but on small provocation, or among · people whose love and sympathy she could count upon, her whimsicality became apparent when she was quite young. She showed this variability of mood, it seems, in after years, and it explains, perhaps, the diverse opinions of her quoted by Mary Russell Mitford, author of *Our Village*, whose mother was a friend of the Austens. Mrs. Mitford says of Jane : " She was then the prettiest, silliest, most affected, husband-hunting butterfly she ever remembers," while a friend describes her as being " . . . perpendicular, precise, taciturn, a poker of whom everyone is afraid."

But, in speaking of husband-hunting, one is anticipating. For us Jane is still more or less in the schoolroom, and, when not busy with her studies, is trying her hand at authorship. The earliest known productions seem to have been written when she was between the ages of fifteen and seventeen. They are plays and stories, slight and deliberately nonsensical, but marked with an impish wit and a precocious sense of irony. All of them are prefaced with a mock-solemn dedication. There is a story called " Evelyn," written in a manuscript book entitled " Volume the Third," and described by Jane as " Effusions of Fancy by a very Young Lady, consisting of Tales in a Style entirely new." This is dedicated " of permission to Miss Mary Lloyd." Another story is entitled, " Adventures of Mr. Harley, dedicated to Francis William Austen, Esq., Midshipman on board his Majesty's Ship *Perseverance*." While a play called " The Mystery," an unfinished comedy, bears on its title-page :

" *To the Rev. George Austen.*

" Sir, - I humbly solicit your patronage to the following Comedy, which, though an unfinished one, is, I flatter myself, as complete a *Mystery* as any of its kind.

"I am, Sir, your most humble Servant,

"THE AUTHOR."

The characters include Mrs. Humbug, Old Humbug, Daphne, and Corydon. There are three scenes, of only a few lines each, and at the quickly reached end of the First Act is scrawled "FINIS."

This truncated drama is included in the recently published collection of Jane's juvenilia entitled : *Volume the First.*

Other manuscripts have been collected by Mrs. Sanders, a descendant of the Austen family, and were published, under the title *Love and Freindship,* in 1922.

In them the note is still one of burlesque and nonsense. They are very entertaining. The book includes the " History of England from the Reign of Henry the 4th to the Death of Charles the 1st. By a Partial, Prejudiced, and Ignorant Historian." Its manner can be judged by these extracts :

" *Edward the 5th.*

"This unfortunate Prince lived so little a while that nobody had him to draw his picture. He was murdered by his Uncle's Contrivance, whose name was Richard the 3rd."

" *Elizabeth.*

" It was the peculiar misfortune of this Woman to have bad Ministers – Since wicked as she herself was, she could not have committed such extensive mischeif, had not these vile and abandoned Men connived at, and encouraged her in her Crimes."

" *James the 1st.*

" Though the King had some faults, among which and as the most principal, was his allowing his Mother's death, yet considered on the whole I cannot help liking him."

Jane's was, as you see, a very personal view of history. Its manner is somewhat similar to that modern extravagance *1066 and All That*, while *Love and Freindship* inevitably recalls Miss Daisy Ashford's *The Young Visiters*, though Jane's work was more sophisticated. It was a deliberate burlesque of certain novels of her day, and may be termed, in some sense, a forerunner of *Northanger Abbey*, in which she set out to caricature the school of fiction of which Mrs. Radcliffe was the leader.

Love and Freindship has been widely read, but it deserves an even wider audience, for it is a delightfully absurd affair. Written in the form of letters, it recounts the experiences of Laura, who thus introduces herself :

" My Father was a native of Ireland and an inhabitant of Wales ; my Mother was the natural daughter of a Scotch Peer by an Italian Opera-girl – I was born in Spain and received my Education at a Convent in France."

This cosmopolitan heroine endures a surprising series of adventures, among a riot of misfortune, accident, bereavement, and the most astounding of coincidences, in a brief space of time. Her companion in distress is one Sophia, much given to fainting, a proclivity shared by Laura, of which she bitterly repents, as her dying words testify :

" Beware of swoons, Dear Laura. . . . A frenzy fit is not one quarter so pernicious ; it is an exercise to the Body and if not so violent, is I dare say conducive to Health in its consequences – Run mad as often as you chuse ; but do not faint."

Another remarkable character is Lord St. Clair, who, at an inn in Scotland, encountered four hitherto unknown grandchildren in the space of a few minutes, the last to be introduced declaring :

" ' I am the son of Agatha your Laurina's 4th
and youngest Daughter.'   'I see you are indeed,' replied Lord St. Clair – 'But tell me
(continued he looking fearfully towards the
Door) tell me, have I any other Grand-children
in the House?'   'None, my Lord.'   'Then
I will provide for you all without delay – Here
are 4 Banknotes of £50 each – Take them and
remember I have done the Duty of a Grandfather.'   He instantly left the Room and immediately afterwards the House."

Which is not to be wondered at, though Laura
was distinctly upset, for she continues :

" You may imagine how greatly we were
surprised by the sudden departure of Lord
St. Clair.   'Ignoble Grand-sire!' exclaimed
Sophia.   'Unworthy Grandfather!' said I,
and instantly fainted in each other's arms."

This admirable tale was dedicated by Jane to
her cousin, Madame la Comtesse de Feuillade,
and is dated 13th June, 1790. She and her husband were then once more in England, whence
they had fled from the first turbulences of the
Revolution. A fact which was possibly to the
Comte de Feuillade's disadvantage, for any

CA

relations with England were suspect. At all
events, on his return to France in 1792, he was
charged with *incivism*, denounced to the Comité
de Salut Publique, and two years later was
guillotined.

Meanwhile, his wife remained in England, and
renewed her intimacy with the Austens, with
whom she had been a frequent correspondent
during the years of her marriage, when she lived
in Paris and on the estates of her husband in
Guyenne. She was a clever woman, vivacious,
amusing, definitely of the world, and, to the inhabitants of Steventon Rectory, must have
seemed an exotic. But no doubt her tales of life
at the Court of Louis XVI and Marie Antoinette,
her enthusiasms for fashion and gaiety, enthralled
her aunt and her cousins. And one may imagine
her amusingly contrasting the artificial pastorals
of *Le Petit Trianon* with the genuine pastorals of
Hampshire. No doubt she brought to Jane
knowledge of certain sides of life which, though
only hearsay, widened her outlook and her interests, and if never directly made use of in her
novels, had its value in her estimates of society.
But the Comtesse was not the sole member of the
Steventon circle who had experience of the Con-
tinent, for Edward Austen, at the expense of his
uncle, Thomas Knight, who had practically

adopted him when a young man, had gone on
the Grand Tour, which had included a visit to
Rome and a year at Dresden.

Elizabeth de Feuillade must have been a
woman of volatile temperament, though possibly
one should not take too seriously her remark when,
three years after de Feuillade's execution, she
married Jane's brother, Henry, that " though she
was not unwilling to marry again she was loth to
give up dear liberty and dearer flirtation." Certainly she had adaptability, for she adjusted her
life with equanimity, and the contrast between
the Court of Versailles and Steventon Rectory
must have been marked. She was, however, a
woman of warm affections, and Jane was always
a favourite with her.

In 1791 she writes of Cassandra and Jane with,
perhaps, more enthusiasm than accuracy. " The
two sisters are perfect beauties. They are two of
the prettiest girls in England." And a year later,
" Cassandra and Jane are both very much grown
and greatly improved in manners as in person.
They are, I think, equally sensible and both so to
a degree seldom met with, but my heart still gives
the preference to Jane." This was natural, for
whatever Cassandra's qualities of character might
have been, Jane's humour and wit must inevitably
have appealed to Elizabeth de Feuillade's nature.

One pictures them having the most amusing and interminable conversations, Jane all eagerness, with her perceptive and enquiring mind, to listen, Eliza, telling of foible and fashion, delighted at finding so sensitive an audience.

Another friend who came into Jane's life at about this time was Anne Lefroy, wife of the rector of Ashe, a small village not far from Steventon. She was a woman of considerable charm, goodness of character, and intelligence, and, though many years older than Jane, they had a deep affection for one another, which was maintained until 1804 when Mrs. Lefroy was killed by a fall from her horse. An event which later prompted Jane to write a sincere, but undistinguished, poem to her memory.

Madame Lefroy, as she was called alike by friends and the villagers of Ashe, was a sister of Sir Egerton Brydges, who, in his autobiography, writes : " The nearest neighbours of the Lefroys were the Austens of Steventon. I remember Jane Austen, the novelist, as a little child. She was very intimate with Mrs. Lefroy, and was much encouraged by her. . . . When I knew Jane Austen I never suspected she was an authoress ; but my eyes told me she was fair and handsome, slight and elegant, but with cheeks a little too full."

This description recalls the portrait by Zoffany

which is said to represent Jane when a girl. The artist has painted his subject with one foot forward, so that she appears almost on tip-toe. She wears a high-waisted muslin dress, and carries a furled sunshade. The face, young and immature, has about it an engaging eagerness, and, though without marked beauty, has marked charm. The eyes are dark and direct, while about the curve of the lips is a hint of that whimsicality on which Philadelphia Walter remarked.

One would like to think this portrait is authentic, in which case it would probably have been painted in 1790, when Jane was fifteen and staying at Bath. The authors of the *Life and Letters* accept it, but other authorities are sceptical. Certainly it seems a little surprising that any member of the Austen family should have gone to the expense of having Jane's portrait painted by an artist so eminent as Zoffany. On the other hand, a certain Dr. Newman of Oxford, when bequeathing the picture to one of the Rice family, who were connections of the Austens, categorically states : " It is a portrait of Jane Austen, the novelist, by Zoffany." Though why this otherwise unknown Dr. Newman should have owned the picture is obscure. Indeed, the whole question is somewhat of a puzzle, though it is pleasant to think there may exist to-day a portrait of Jane in her girlhood ; for apart from this picture and a sketch made by her sister, Cassandra – and lost, since an engraving was made from it in 1870 – there is no portrait of Jane known. The visitor at the National Portrait Gallery enquires in vain.

Life at Steventon, if without variety, had its incidents, chiefly occasioned by the coming and going of one or other of the brothers, of relations, Austens, Knights, and Leighs, and the visits of friends. Letters were always an interest, and there was a constant interchange of family news by post. Mr. Austen, in a letter to Francis on joining his first ship, the *Perseverance*, urges the boy to write frequently, and assures him : " You may depend on hearing from us at every opportunity." This is a letter, too long to quote, which, admirably illustrating Mr. Austen's nature, combines good sense and persuasively given advice as to behaviour, and is a rare example of gentle affection and parental wisdom. Behind the written words is a strong feeling of religion.

This always prevailed in the Austen household. But it was a religion practised without austerity or compulsion, it being accepted gladly and without question as the underlying basis of life, the importance of which required neither being stressed nor ignored. Certainly it was free from pietistic exaggeration, just as it was from doubt or hesitation. At Steventon the speculations of Continental thought were probably unconsidered if not unknown. Elizabeth de Feuillade might mention Monsieur Voltaire, the Encyclopædists, and the rest, but their opinions would be outside Mr. Austen's serious thought, and certainly not likely to capture the interest of the youthful Jane. Her faith was that of her parents and her brothers. It remained unshaken, unquestioned, though unobtrusive, to the end of her life.

Her staunch Christianity, however, did not preclude her from sarcastic references to the contemporary state of the Church in more than one of her novels, where she speaks of the Church as a facile and lazy profession for younger sons. " Seven hundred a year is a fine thing for a younger brother . . . and a sermon at Christmas and Easter, I suppose, will be the sum total of sacrifice," Crawford remarks in *Mansfield Park*. But the other side of the matter is given in the same book, where Edmund Bertram stoutly defends the clergy against Miss Crawford's acrid criticisms. Here, as always, Jane saw both points of view, though not invariably did her heart gain the better of her judgment and allow her to utter them.

Certainly Mr. Austen's duties were not arduous, but he did not neglect them, and one need not take

seriously the accusation that, because it was sometimes his custom to read poetry aloud in the
mornings, he was indolent. When his sons had
gone into the world, and the expenses of the
growing family no longer made it necessary for
him to take pupils, he would have had ample
leisure. For his cure was a very small one, and
his twin parishes did not contain more than three
hundred inhabitants.

The church of Deane has been totally rebuilt
since George Austen's time, but the church at
Steventon, at least outwardly, remains as it was.
It is situated about half a mile from the site of the
Rectory, whence it was reached by a path known
in Jane's day as "The Church Walk." It is a small
plain affair, its walls now coated with grey plaster,
with, at its western end, a square tower bearing a
stumpy, slated steeple. To-day the visitor gains
admission after finding an enormous key in the
cleft of a yew-tree which grows in the graveyard.
Within, the church is narrow and dark, lit by
Early English windows. It has been rigorously
restored. There are deal pews, bad glass, and
some Victorian frescoes, gently fading to a well-
merited obscurity. Several memorials to Austens
and Knights are to be seen, including one to Anne,
the wife of Jane's brother, James, who died in
1795.

But though an uninspiring little building, Steventon Church is well placed. From the level hill-top, which it shares with Steventon Manor – quite recently greatly enlarged – one has a wide view, and one can appreciate the mild, homely landscape which Jane loved, and knew so intimately. It is a landscape entirely without emphasis. The land rises and falls unobtrusively. There are no deep valleys or conspicuous hills. The fields of pasture or of tilth, together with the frequent copses, make a diversely coloured and intricate pattern. The copses are of hazel and moderate-sized oaks. Elms grow in the hedgerows, where, in spring, the earth is covered with thickly clustered primroses, wood-anemones, and violets.

One may picture Jane wandering in these fields, and the lanes that wind between the gently folded hills, taking those walks which were the pleasure of the majority of her heroines. In summer, with their sunshades raised, leisurely, indolently pursuing their way ; in winter, with pattens and umbrellas, defying the lowering skies and the slanting rain. And she, as they, would chatter to her companions – for rarely would they be alone – of friends and neighbours, of incipient or ripened love-affairs, of dinners, of hoped-for balls, of fashion and scandal. And

Jane, one thinks, would, to the chosen confidante, Elizabeth de Feuillade, Anna Lefroy, or the beloved Cassandra, have talked of other, deeper things, never expressed in her novels, nor in the letters which have been preserved to us ; searching for understanding of the human comedy, an angle of which she knew so intimately, and whose protagonists she could draw with both a tender and an acid fidelity. Many subjects she must have discussed in those years at Steventon, many timid speculations she must have made, and many imaginings have come to her restless, searching mind. But it is certain that she would never have contemplated the possibility that nearly a hundred and fifty years later lovers of her work would visit the scene of her childhood, youth, and early maturity, for her sake. Had the notion been presented to her, she would have laughed at and ridiculed it, and possibly been a little disturbed. For she was a humble creature.

CHAPTER II

1788–1800

By 1788, in which year Jane paid her first visit
to London, and afterwards went to stay with her
uncle, Francis Austen, at Sevenoaks, the majority
of her brothers had gone into the world. James,
the eldest, after being a scholar of St. John's College, Oxford, had been ordained and become a
curate at Overton, near Steventon ; Henry, also
a scholar of St. John's, was vacillating about his
future career, which was to prove so diverse ;
Francis, in H.M.S. *Perseverance*, was stationed in
the East Indies ; Edward was living in Kent, with
the Knights ; Charles was still at home, a boy of
nine. And so, presumably, was the invalid and
ignored George.

A little later there were two weddings in the
family, Edward, in 1791, marrying Elizabeth
Bridges, the daughter of a Kentish knight ; and
James, in 1792, Anne, daughter of General and
Lady Jane Mathew, of Laverstoke, in Hampshire.
Soon Mrs. Austen could boast of those grand-
children (whose descendants were to become, in

rather a confusing fashion, Knights, Austens, Leighs, and Austen-Leighs) to whom we owe so much information concerning their aunt.

At about this time – the mid-nineties of the century – Jane wrote *Lady Susan*, a novel in letter form, a manner popular since the days of Samuel Richardson's *Pamela*, and favoured by Jane for some years. For, as we have seen, she employed it in more than one of her juvenilia, and later the original draft of *Sense and Sensibility* was to be written in letters. *Lady Susan* is unfinished, and there is no indication why it was laid aside. Possibly, after the initial interest, the theme did not please her, and certainly it is a somewhat curious one for Jane to have chosen for her first attempt at serious authorship. It is in many ways quite unlike her other work, for not only does the chief character dominate the story, in a way which she never repeated, but the character of Lady Susan is of a type which Jane never sought to draw again. She is a middle-aged woman – or rather what in those days would be considered middle-aged, when youth was not indefinitely suspended as it now is – of an ambitious, unscrupulous, and vicious nature. In short, she is a Georgian " vamp," and, on the whole, a very able portrait of the species, though her inveterate self-seeking and ambition do not perfectly convince in spite of the vitality of its presentation.

The choice of a heroine of this sort, rather than either the persecuted maidens to be found in the novels of Mrs. Radcliffe, or the sentimental ones like those to be found in the novels of Fanny Burney, shows that Jane had a decided independence of thought in avoiding that imitativeness usual among fledgling writers of fiction. The less important persons of the story are sketched more lightly, but the whole strikes the reader as being written with complete conviction, and contrives to give a vivid idea of the characters without the aid of description, or of that dialogue which is so important a factor in Jane's achievement.

Miss Mary Austen-Leigh in her book *Personal Aspects of Jane Austen*, published in 1920, suggests that the theme of the novel, or rather its protagonist, was drawn from a family manuscript relating to an ancestress of intimate friends of Jane's, who always spoke of her as " the cruel Mrs. ———." The career of this woman was by no means similar to that of the imaginary Lady Susan, but there is a common hardness and inhumanity, mixed with charm and beauty, which might well influence Jane to make her the prototype of Lady Susan, and supports Miss Austen-Leigh's theory. Or perhaps maybe, her cousin, Elizabeth de Feuillade, might have suggested the theme with one of her tales of the French Court. It is even possible that Elizabeth herself was the model for the lighter and more frivolous sides of Lady Susan's character.

The book was given to the public by Jane's nephew, the Rev. J. E. Austen Leigh, who was the author of her first biography, published in 1870. A second edition appeared in the following year, under the title, *Lady Susan, Etc.*, in which this unfinished novel was printed.

In 1882 the original manuscript of the book came into the possession of Lord Brabourne, grandson of Edward (Austen) Knight, on the death of his mother, Lady Knatchbull. And with it Jane's letters to her sister, Cassandra. These were contained in a square box, and, as Lord Brabourne states, were " fastened up carefully in separate packets, each of which was endorsed, ' For Lady Knatchbull,' in the handwriting of my great-aunt, Cassandra Austen, and with which was a paper endorsed, in my mother's handwriting, ' Letters from my dear Aunt Jane Austen, and two from Aunt Cassandra after her decease.' . . . The box itself had been endorsed by my mother as follows : ' Letters from Aunt Jane to Aunt Cassandra at different periods of her life – a few to me – and some from Aunt Cass to me after At. Jane's death.' This endorsement bears the date August 1856, and was probably made the last time my mother looked at the letters."

This correspondence, unknown to Mr. J. E. Austen Leigh, who had only had access to a few letters which had come into the possession of his sisters on Cassandra's death in 1845, threw so many new lights on Jane's private character, her temperament, and her opinions, that Lord Brabourne decided to publish them. But he had some scruples about doing so, for, he says, " they contain the confidential outpourings of Jane Austen's soul to her beloved sister, interspersed with many family and personal details which, doubtless, she would have told to no other human being. But to-day, more than seventy long years have rolled away since the greater part of them were written ; no one living can, I think, have any possible just cause of annoyance at their publication, whilst, if I judge rightly, the public never took a more deeper or more lively interest in all that concerns Jane Austen than at the present moment." Moreover, it was known that Cassandra had taken care to destroy any letters which she deemed should only be read by herself, so Lord Brabourne might safely feel that those which remained had passed her censorship.

He published these inherited letters – they number ninety-four – in 1884, with prefatory chapters dealing with various family matters and some criticism of the novels. Since then, however, a good deal more of Jane's correspondence has come to light, and Dr. R. W Chapman's volume, *Jane Austen's Letters*, published in 1932, contain nearly one hundred and fifty. This is a complete collection, and it is most ably edited and annotated.

The correspondence starts in 1796, and continues to Jane's death in 1817. A very large proportion of these letters are addressed to Cassandra, to whom it was her custom to write fully and frequently whenever they chanced to be separated. Jane's childish love for her sister, which prompted Mrs. Austen to remark, " If Cassandra were going to have her head cut off, Jane would insist upon sharing her fate," increased with the years, and was maintained to the end. It appears to have been a perfect intimacy, founded on a deep understanding of each other's natures, and was undoubtedly a guiding influence in both their lives. Jane clung to her sister to her death, while it seems that, after the anguish of the long fatal illness, Cassandra was most happy in her memories, often speaking of Jane with, as a niece describes it, " such an accent of *living* love in her voice."

But it was a love without morbidness or sentimentality, as the letters prove. There are in them no excessive endearments, no jealousies and complaints. Rather they are an interchange of gossip where nothing is too trivial to record, the writer well aware that the recipient would find nothing too trivial to read. And it is to be imagined that Cassandra would answer them with the same eagerness and interest, though without that acuteness of phrase, that taking of an especial angle of view, that Puckish mischief, so characteristic of Jane. But alas ! there is no trace of Cassandra's side of the correspondence, which probably she herself destroyed.

To some degree in the letters, and certainly to a profound degree in conversation, Cassandra played to Jane the rôle of confessor. To her she expressed herself as she never did in her novels, giving vent to thoughts and emotions of a nature which must have, at the core, had passion, though outwardly it was restrained. As a rule her feet were always on the ground – or should it be the carpet of a drawing-room ? – and seldom did she spread her wings. Only here and there in the novels, and then, half disguised, rarely in the letters, and only fully in her intimacy with

Da

Cassandra, did she speak from the depth of her heart. And then her irrepressible humour would forbid more than a momentary solemnity. For life, in her view, was, primarily, something to be observed, commented upon, but the deeper implications of which it was wiser, for the most part, to ignore. Even with Cassandra her knowledge would be greater than her utterance ; her feeling more profound than her expression. And often she herself must have wondered a little as to both the extent and depth of her comprehensions of life. For though she recognised her limitations, one guesses she was uncertain as to the vastness or smallness of the field of experience and sympathy which lay beyond the boundaries of her imagination.

There is a tradition in the Austen family that " Cassandra had the *merit* of having her temper always under control, but that Jane had the *happiness* of a temper which never required to be commanded." Certainly the sisters were different in disposition. Cassandra was without Jane's impulsiveness and sudden ardours. Her character was more rigid. Though she shared the gift of humour common to the Austens, she had not that sense of nonsense which was so marked in Jane. Cassandra might laugh at her sister's shafts of maliciousness, her whimsical and ironic *obita dicta* ; it would be alien for her to cap or imitate them. But in her rôle of Mother Confessor she would give her applause for wit, equally with compassion and advice, when that was needed. For, in each and every event, Jane could depend on Cassandra, whether the subject of confidence was a new pelisse, a passage in one of the novels, or at that time when Jane suffered not from love unrequited but love destroyed by death. Always she could rely upon her interest, her balanced judgment, and, above all, on her enduring tenderness of heart. Theirs was, it seems, a perfect friendship.

It is idle, but natural, to speculate in what direction Jane's life, and even her genius, would have shaped if, as at one time appeared inevitable, the sisters' paths divided. For, had Cassandra married, however strong the ties of affection between them might have been, Cassandra, with others to share her love, with the duties of a wife and mother, could not have maintained the intimacy which, as things happened, existed between them ; could not, indeed, have devoted her life to her sister. And it is not an exaggeration to say that this is what she did. Jane, comparatively alone, would inevitably have developed differently.

But Cassandra's sole love-affair ended in

tragedy, as, later, Jane's was to do, and so forged another link of sympathy between the sisters.

Thomas Craven Fowle, to whom Cassandra became engaged in 1795, had once been a pupil at Steventon Rectory, and was a few years younger than herself. He had entered the Church, and was in expectation of being given a living by his cousin, Lord Craven ; but until this expectation was realised he could not afford to marry. Meanwhile, Lord Craven had him appointed chaplain of his regiment, with which he sailed to the West Indies. And there, shortly before his anticipated return to England, he died of yellow fever, bequeathing Cassandra a small legacy.

Two other deaths at about this time influenced the Austens. Thomas Knight, who had adopted Edward Austen, died in 1794, leaving him his heir to both the Godmersham and Chawton estates. Three years later, Mrs. Knight made over these properties to him, retaining, however, an income of £2,000 per annum. Soon afterwards, Edward assumed the name of his benefactor. The other death was that of James Austen's wife in 1795, following which, her child, Anna, went to live with her grandparents at Steventon. Jane had a strong affection for her, and later she gave much advice and criticism when Anna herself started novel-writing. She married the Reverend Benjamin Lefroy, who was a cousin of Jane's first authentic admirer.

This was Thomas Lefroy, an Irishman, nephew of Jane's friend, Mrs. Lefroy, of Ashe. He is referred to in a letter, dated January 1796, offering birthday wishes to Cassandra, who was staying with the Fowles at Kintbury. She writes : " In the first place I hope you will live another twenty-three years longer. Mr. Tom Lefroy's birthday was yesterday, so that you are very near of an age. . . . You scold me so much in the nice long letter which I have this moment received from you, that I am almost afraid to tell you how my Irish friend and I behaved. Imagine to yourself everything most profligate and shocking in the way of dancing and sitting down together. I *can* expose myself, however, only *once more*, because he leaves the country after next Friday, on which day we *are* to have a dance at Ashe after all. He is a very gentlemanlike, good-looking, pleasant young man, I assure you. But as to our having met, except at the last three balls, I cannot say much ; for he is so excessively laughed at about me at Ashe, that he is ashamed of coming to Steventon, and ran away when we called on Mrs. Lefroy a few days ago." But her admirer's bashfulness seems to have been overcome on at least one occasion, for, following some gossip, Jane continues : " After I had written the above, we received a visit from Mr. Tom Lefroy and his cousin George. The latter is really very well-behaved now ; and as for the other, he has but *one* fault, which time will, I trust, entirely remove – it is that his morning coat is a great deal too light. He is a very great admirer of Tom Jones, and therefore wears the same coloured clothes, I imagine, which *he* did when he was wounded."

In a letter written a few days later, speaking once more of the ball, Jane says : " I look forward with great impatience to it, as I rather expect to receive an offer from my friend in the course of the evening. I shall refuse him, however, unless he promises to give away his white coat." While, in an addition to the same letter : " At length the day is come on which I am to flirt my last with Tom Lefroy, and when you receive this it will all be over. My tears flow as I write at the melancholy idea."

It is impossible to decide how serious was this flirtation ; how much Jane's mockery of the white coat could be applied to Tom Lefroy himself ; whether or not indeed the proposal of marriage was made at Ashe. It seems probable that it was, for it is said that to the end of his life, Lefroy – he lived to be ninety-two – did not forget his attachment to Jane ; which looks as if on his side it was serious. But he does not appear to have been an insistent lover, and once having had his refusal, given perhaps with a not really intentioned lightness and raillery, he held aloof ; while Jane, piqued maybe, let the matter drop. Only once again does she allude to him in her letters. This was two years later, when, after a visit from Mrs. Lefroy, she says : " Of her nephew she said nothing at all, and of her friend very little. She did not once mention the former to *me*, and I was too proud to make any enquiries ; but on my father's afterwards asking where he was, I learnt that he was gone back to London on his way to Ireland, where he is called to the Bar and means to practise." Which he did with success, for he eventually became Lord Chief Justice of Ireland.

In the October of the year when Jane danced at Ashe, she began to write *Pride and Prejudice*, originally entitled " First Impressions." Probably by this time the sisters had the sitting-room of their own which Anna Austen many years after described. It was called " ' the dressing-room ' . . . perhaps because it opened into a smaller chamber in which my two aunts slept. I remember the common-looking carpet with its chocolate ground, and the painted press with shelves above for books, and Jane's piano, and an

oval glass that hung between the windows ; but
the charm of the room, with its scanty furniture
and cheaply-papered walls, must have been, for
those old enough to understand it, the flow of
native household wit, with all the fun and nonsense of a large and clever family."

Certainly Anna was not old enough in those
days to appreciate what her Aunt Jane was writing, but she was sufficiently acute to remember
the names of the characters and repeat them to
her grandparents. And be reprimanded in consequence, for the book was at that time a secret.
How long it remained so we do not know, but
three months after the book was finished, in
August 1797, Mr. Austen approached the London
publisher, Cadell, in the following terms.

" SIR, – I have in my possession a manuscript
novel, comprising 3 vols., about the length of
Miss Burney's *Evelina*. As I am well aware of
what consequence it is that a work of this sort
should make its first appearance under a re-
spectable name, I apply to you. I shall be
much obliged, therefore, if you will inform me
whether you choose to be concerned in it, what
will be the expense of publishing it at the
author's risk, and what you will venture to
advance for the property of it, if on perusal it

is approved of? Should you give any encouragement, I will send you the work.

" I am, Sir, your humble servant,

" GEORGE AUSTEN.

" Steventon, Overton, Hants.

" *November 1, 1797.*"

But Mr. Cadell gave no encouragement. On the contrary, he refused the offer by return of post. And it was not until fourteen years later that *Pride and Prejudice* was published. By which time it had been subjected to more than one revision, so that it is not possible to determine how the original draft, written in the " dressing-room " at Steventon, compares with the novel which we read to-day. Certainly there are in it few signs of immaturity, and though there is an added tenderness and mellowness of judgment in Jane's last works, *Mansfield Park* and *Persuasion*, the first has nothing of the tentativeness of the novice. The wit and observation displayed are not surpassed in any of the other novels. The characterisation is sure. Indeed, the definitely " comic " characters, Mrs. Bennett, Mr. Collins, and that superb snob, Lady Catherine de Bourgh, surely eclipse Miss Bates, the intolerable Mrs. Norris and the rest? Moreover, there is Mr. Bennett, an original and subtle study, while Elizabeth Bennett is one of the most engaging of Jane's heroines. She has humour, charm, and, on the whole, great good sense, and one may well disclaim the assertion made by, among others, Sir Walter Scott, that her affection for Darcy was considerably influenced by her visit to spacious Pemberley. A preposterous notion ! Of Darcy himself opinions may well be divided. He is not an entirely sympathetic character. He could be both stiff and arrogant, and for too long, perhaps, one feels that his head ruled his heart. But he is more distinct, more an individual, than others of Jane's heroes, and wedded to the enchanting Elizabeth one feels assured that he became not only an admirable husband, but a likeable man.

The narrative is throughout beautifully contrived, while the scenes shift easily and naturally to a greater variety of environments than is usual in Jane's work. Longbourn, Netherfield Park, Hunsford, Pemberley itself ; the atmosphere of all these places is indicated with an exquisite economy and precision. And equally so are the small differences in social status of the various characters.

Jane, it appears, was not disheartened by Mr. Cadell's curt refusal even to consider her manuscript, for in the same month that her father wrote to him, she began another novel, first written in the form of letters and called "Elinor and Marianne." Later to be recast, renamed *Sense and Sensibility*, and eventually to be the first of her published works.

In this same year, Henry Austen – who had joined the Oxford Militia in 1793 and was now captain and adjutant – married his widowed cousin, Elizabeth de Feuillade. His was to be a varied career, and it is difficult to associate the Militia officer, husband of the somewhat frivolous Comtesse, with the earnest evangelical preacher which he was eventually to become, after spending many years in London, where in 1802 he set up as a banker and army agent in partnership with another Militia officer named Maunde.

He was without doubt Jane's favourite brother. He had his share of the Austen good looks, and, at any rate in early life, was a man of a singularly happy and optimistic temperament. (Perhaps too optimistic, for, his banking exploit was to end in disaster and bankruptcy.) Like Jane he was a brilliant conversationalist, and like her delighted in a wayward and satiric form of humour. He, most of all the family, appreciated those arrows of wit with which, in her novels, she pierces her characters ; those acute observations and comments that appear both in her fiction and in her letters, and must often have enlivened her talk.

He, though Cassandra was " a good listener,"
must have been the most responsive member of
her immediate audience. It is to be deplored that
there exist none of the letters which she must have
written to him.

But if Henry was the favourite, Jane was
strongly attached to all her brothers. She fol-
lowed the careers in the Navy of Francis and
Charles with an ardent interest throughout her
life ; and she had a deep affection for Edward,
who, though without the brilliance, the literary
taste and scholarship of Henry, was a man possessed of great kindness of heart and charm of
manner. One imagines, indeed, that she was on
excellent terms with them all, and, to the end,
discussed with them not only the affairs of the
family, but affairs in general without restraint.
Probably from these discussions she gleaned a
wider view of life than could have been obtained
from observation alone, and one guesses there
would be few subjects she would not debate
with them – certainly where Henry was concerned. For Jane, though decorous, was no
prude. She always faced facts ; but if they did
not interest or amuse her she ignored them.

She was by this time twenty-two years old, and
enjoyed a certain independence. She stayed here
and there with friends, she visited Bath, and,

when at home, she moved freely in the somewhat limited society of the neighbourhood. She was a fond and exquisite dancer, and joyfully attended the balls held during the winter at the Basingstoke Assembly Rooms, and those at various country houses. She speaks from her heart when she wrote in *Emma*, " It may be possible to do without dancing entirely. Instances have been known of young people passing many, many months successively, without being at a ball of any description, and no material injury accrue either to body or mind ; but when a beginning is made – when the felicities of rapid motion have once been, though slightly, felt – it must be a very heavy set that does not ask for more."

Only a short time before Jane's days it was the custom – which strikes one as curiously modern – for a lady to have only one partner throughout the evening, but this fashion had lapsed, and one may imagine her as being eagerly sought for in reel, hornpipe, country-dance, which dance was at this date very popular, or in the still greatly favoured minuet. For if she was not strictly beautiful, she was, as her nephew, J. E. Austen Leigh, asserts, " very attractive," tall and slender, her step light and firm, and her whole appearance expressive of health and animation. In complexion she was a clear brunette with a rich

colour ; she had full round cheeks, with mouth
and nose small and well-formed, bright hazel
eyes, and brown hair forming natural curls close
round her face. And if one wonders what the
young men who were her partners thought of the
whimsical and barbed criticisms of other persons
in the ball-room which must surely have passed
her lips – unless they were reserved for Cassandra
in the privacy of the dressing-room – certainly she
seldom sat out a dance. For on one occasion she
writes : " There were twenty dances and I danced
them all." And on another : " I danced nine
dances out of ten," in spite of " a scarcity of men
in general, and a still greater scarcity of any that
were much good."

In 1798, Mrs. Knight left Godmersham Park ;
upon which fact Jane afterwards commented
somewhat spitefully, saying : " It was no such
prodigious act of generosity after all, it seems, for
she preserved herself an income out of it still ; this
ought to be known, that her conduct may not
be overrated. I rather think Edward shows the
most magnanimity of the two, in accepting her
resignation with such encumbrances." But it
should be remembered that Mrs. Knight was
under no obligation to allow Edward Austen
(now Edward Knight) benefit under his uncle's
will until her death. However that may be,

Edward left Rowling, where hitherto he had lived, and moved to Godmersham.

This property is situated in the valley of the Stour, about eight miles from Canterbury. An engraving in Hasted's *Kent* shows it in 1784 as a large stone house with two wings, settled in a valley, the river winding through the park, and behind it a hill on which was the Temple Plantation, called by Jane " a Chevalier Bayard of a plantation."

Throughout her life she often stayed here, and Godmersham brought her a host of new friends and acquaintances, who are referred to, a quite bewildering number of names, in the letters which she wrote from Kent. It is the same in her letters from Steventon and elsewhere, and we owe much to Dr. Chapman, who has painstakingly identified the various persons constantly mentioned. Jane knew indeed – except in the last years at Chawton, where she did not move much in the local society – a large number of people, and their lives and occupations take up a great deal of space in her correspondence.

There is a constant going to and fro, in curricles, gigs, and barouches, of friends who visit one another either to dine, or merely to gossip over a glass of wine. In those days the morning call was in vogue, and there are frequent instances of them

in the novels. They remained so, indeed, for
many years. (The curious may learn of the correct behaviour on these occasions in a book,
entitled *Domestic Duties, or Advice to Young Married
Ladies*, first published in 1824, where the authoress,
though admitting " they fritter away so much
time," declares " morning visits cannot be very
well dispensed with.")   There were evening par-
ties, with dancing, music, or cards. Jane joined
in all of these amusements, and in her letters to
Cassandra not only recounted what she had done
but whom she had met, until there emerges from
the pages of her correspondence a large gallery of
portraits, lively and human as are the characters of
her fiction.   Some are full-lengths, drawn in detail ; others mere sketches ; some, perhaps, should
be called caricatures.   For instance : " Mrs. Hall
of Sherborne, was brought to bed yesterday of a
dead child, some weeks before she expected, owing
to a fright.   I suppose she unawares happened to
look at her husband."   " Mr. Gould . . . walked
home with me after Tea ; he is a very young
Man, just entered of Oxford, wears Spectacles, &
has heard that *Evelina* was written by Dr. Johnson."   " Mrs. Blount appeared exactly as she did
in September, with the same broad face, diamond
bandeau, white shoes, pink husband, & fat
neck."   " Mrs. Powlett at once expensively and

nakedly dressed." " Dear Mrs. Digweed ! – I
cannot bear that she sh^d not be foolishly happy
after a Ball." And finally : " Mr. Rob. Mascall
breakfasted here ; he eats a great deal of Butter."

But it must not be supposed that Jane always
took this satiric way – so often the easiest – in
drawing her sketches ; and, even when she did,
one feels that the satire is mischievous rather than
malicious. She was not, at heart, a good hater.
She did not even really despise the most ridiculous, either of her creations or her acquaintances.
But she could seldom resist her favourite weapons,
nonsense and irony. And she was always prepared to turn them upon herself.

Everything is looked at through her quizzing-
glass, and it is always set in her own particular
focus. " What dreadful Hot weather we have ! "
she exclaims, and adds : " It keeps one in a con-
tinual state of Inelegance ! " She is allowed to
undertake certain domestic duties, and says : " I
am very grand indeed ; I had the dignity of
dropping out my mother's laudanum last night.
I carry about the keys of the wine and closet, and
twice since I began this letter have had orders to
give in the kitchen." She mentions Mrs. Austen :
" My mother continues hearty, her appetite &
nights are very good, but her Bowels are still
not entirely settled, & she sometimes complains

E A

of an Asthma, a Dropsy, Water in her Chest & a Liver Disorder." And she ends her delighted account of how a certain Admiral Gambier has used his influence to give Charles Austen promotion, with : " There ! I may now finish my letter and go and hang myself, for I am sure I can neither write nor do anything which will not appear insipid to you after this."

For, in spite of the sharpness of her thoughts and her words, she was not heartless. When it was meet, she had both reverence and humility, and she knew when fun was out of place. But that was not often.

Sir Leslie Stephen asserted that Jane's letters are trivial. That is a narrow view of them. Certainly they deal with trivial matters. There is much chatter about dress, mantles, tippets, caps, and the rest ; there are frequent lists of what was had for dinner – slightly reminiscent of the gargantuan meals detailed with such gusto by the voracious Parson Woodforde – there is much of what may be called " tittle-tattle." But everything bears the stamp of Jane's mind, everything is viewed from her angle. She makes the reader share to the full whatever incident she describes. With the result that she paints her own portrait with the same fidelity that she employed on Emma or Anne Elliot. Touch after touch is added, whether it be such a saying as, " I am still a Cat if I see a Mouse," or, " You know how interesting the purchase of a spongecake is to me."

And always when reading the letters one has the feeling of the sympathy that existed not only between Jane and Cassandra, but with all the Austens. It is like being a privileged listener to the flow of talk in a happy family circle, with its banter, its human interests, its jokes, its deep, but never sentimentally stressed, affection. Most of the Austens, it would seem, appreciated Jane's opinions, her reactions to this or that event, her comment on this or that person, and they were bound together with mutual understanding and mutual laughter.

And, apart from the human interest of the letters, they give a clear, detailed insight into the life of the upper middle-class of the time which is very valuable for its accuracy and detail. Reading them, we become intimately acquainted with the surroundings, the manner of living, and the general outlook of country squires and parsons, and their ladies. We learn how they dressed, how they behaved, what they ate, what were their amusements, what their sports. All these matters are presented vividly and eagerly. But of the world in general, it is true, we learn little. There is not much more allusion to the great happenings

of the times than there is in the novels. Jane was
absorbed in the Human Comedy as she knew it
in drawing-rooms and lush parks. She seldom
ventured into reference to the vast Inhuman
Comedy which was being played in Europe during
these years. But that does not necessarily mean
that she was either ignorant or callous in regard
to it.

Sense and Sensibility was finished in 1798, but
Jane appears to have made no steps to secure its
publication. Probably she was disheartened after
the curt refusal of her previous work. But whether
her work was published or not did not deter her
from writing, for within a few months of finish-
ing *Sense and Sensibility* she began *Northanger Abbey*.
But progress ·with it was slower than with the
other two novels, and it was not completed until
1803, by which time the Austens had left
Steventon.

There, life continued as usual, with a coming
and going of brothers and friends. The customary
visits to neighbouring houses were paid, walks
taken (she alludes to herself and her friend,
Martha Lloyd, of Ibthorp, as being " desperate
walkers "), dresses and caps were altered as the
fashions changed ; books were read ; and her
books were written.

In the letters, family news, such as Francis

being promoted to be Commander, and appointed
to the sloop *Peterel* at Gibraltar, alternates with
such domestic items as the following : " Dame
Tilbury washes for us no more, as Sukey has got
a place. John Stevens' wife undertakes our
purification. She does not look as if anything she
touched would ever be clean, but who knows ? "
On a Sunday evening, she writes : " We have
had a dreadful storm of wind in the forepart of
the day this day, which has done a great deal of
mischief among our trees. – I was sitting alone in
the dining-room, when an odd kind of crash
startled me – in a moment afterwards it was
repeated ; I then went to the window, which I
reached just in time to see the last of our two
highly valued Elms descend into the Sweep ! ! ! ! !
. . . I am happy to add however that no greater
Evil than the loss of Trees has been the consequence of the Storm in this place, or in our
immediate neighbourhood. – We grieve therefore
in some comfort."   The Lefroys at Ashe suffered
more, for, in a letter written a little later, we
learn that : " We sat down 14 to dinner in the
study, the dining-room being not habitable from
the Storm's having blown down its chimney."
At this party : " Mrs. Bramston talked a great
deal of nonsense which Mr. Bramston & Mr.
Clerk seemed almost equally to enjoy. – There

was a whist & casino table, & six outsiders. – Rice
& Lucy made love, Mat : Robinson fell asleep,
James & Mrs. Augustus alternately read Dr.
Jenner's pamphlet on the cow pox, & I bestowed
my company by turns on all."

In May of 1799, Jane and Mrs. Austen paid
another visit to Bath, with her brother Edward
and his wife. Her first letter after arrival is more
than usually vivacious, and reads as if Jane was
enjoying herself to the full. That was her way,
for, as she once observed, " I do not think it worth
while to wait for enjoyment until there is some
real opportunity for it."

" We are exceedingly pleased with the house,"
she writes. " Mrs. Bromley is a fat woman in
mourning, and a little black kitten runs about the
staircase . . . we have two nice-sized rooms,
with dirty quilts, and everything comfortable. . . .
There was a very long list of arrivals in the news-
paper yesterday, so that we need not immediately
dread absolute solitude ; and there is a public
breakfast in Sydney Gardens every morning, so
that we shall not be wholly starved."

In this and the following letters we have an
admirable account of her stay at Bath. We learn
that Edward bathes at the Hetling Pump and
tries Electricity ; that Jane buys a Cloak costing
not quite two pounds, and remarks that in

millinery : "Flowers are very much worn, & Fruit
is still more the thing. Eliz : has a bunch of
Strawberries, & I have seen Grapes, Cherries,
Plumbs & Apricots. – There are likewise Almonds
& raisins, french plumbs & Tamarinds at the
Grocers, but I have never seen any of them in
hats." The party takes walks, attends two galas
in Sydney Gardens with illuminations and fire-
works, and encounters several friends and relations.

Among the latter were the Leigh Perrotts.
Mrs. Perrott was Mrs. Austen's only sister. Later
in the year this lady was to undergo a most dis-
turbing experience, being accused of shoplifting.
The Times of 8th August gives the following
account :

> " The Lady of a gentleman at Bath, possessed
> of a good fortune, and respected by a numerous
> circle of acquaintance, was committed on
> Thursday by G. Chapman, Esq., the Major,
> to the County Gaol at Ilchester, on a charge
> of privately stealing a card of lace from a
> haberdasher's shop."

Mrs. Perrott was not, in fact, sent to gaol, but
was lodged in an adjacent house, and the dis-
tracted Mr. Perrott, vowing that if his wife were

convicted he would follow her to transportation, moved to Ilchester, to be near his wife until the trial, which did not take place until the March of the next year. The event naturally greatly perturbed the Austens, and Mrs. Austen was so distressed that she offered to send Cassandra and Jane to Ilchester to console the wretched prisoner. This offer, however, was not accepted. And the whole affair ended happily, for Mrs. Perrott was acquitted, it being presumed that the haberdasher had acted from some unknown motives of spite, and had inserted a length of black lace into a parcel of white lace which Mrs. Perrott had purchased, and taken with her from the shop.

But the affair had some importance for the Austens, as many years later when Mr. Perrott died, he did not, as had been anticipated, bequeath a legacy to his sister-in-law, but left everything to his wife, as evidence – a little self-conscious and unnecessary – that he had implicit faith in her integrity.

CHAPTER III

1800–1809

In the autumn of 1800, Mr. Austen, for reasons of health and advancing age, decided to leave Steventon, installing his son, James, at the Rectory, and handing over to him the care of the parish.

The matter had been discussed for some time, but Jane does not appear to have taken it very seriously, for when she returned from a visit and Mrs. Austen announced to herself and Cassandra : " Well, girls, it is all settled. We have decided to leave Steventon and to go to Bath," the decision was so unexpected that Jane promptly fainted – a habit unusual with her, however popular it might have been with her contemporaries.

But a few weeks later, she had accustomed herself to the idea – either philosophically, or finding that, on second thoughts, it was not after all so distasteful – for she writes of plans with her expected mixture of common sense and nonsense. " My Mother looks forward with as much certainty as you can do, to our keeping two Maids –

my father is the only one not in the secret. – We plan having a steady Cook, & a young giddy Housemaid, with a sedate, middle aged Man, who is to undertake the double office of Husband to the former & sweetheart to the latter. – No children of course to be allowed on either side."

She discusses in detail the various streets of Bath where they might live, and then follows a list of pictures, " the Battle peice, Mr. Nibbs, Sir Wm. East, & all the heterogeneous, miscellany, manuscript, Scriptoral peices " dispersed about the house which are to be left to the, probably, unwilling James. And then : " My father & mother wisely aware of the difficulty of finding in all Bath such a bed as their own, have resolved on taking it with them. . . . I do not think it will be worth while to remove any of our chests of Drawers. – We shall be able to get some of the most commodious form, made of deal, & painted to look very neat ; & I flatter myself that for little comforts of all kinds, our apartment will be one of the most complete things of the sort all over Bath – Bristol included." She ends her letter : " I get more & more reconciled to the idea of our removal. We have lived long enough in this Neighbourhood, and the Basingstoke Balls are certainly on the decline, there is something inter-esting in the bustle of going away, & the prospect

of spending future summers by the Sea or in
Wales is very delightful. – For a time we shall now
possess many of the advantages which I have
often thought of with Envy in the wives of Sailors
or Soldiers. – It must not be generally known
however that I am not sacrificing a great deal in
quitting the Country – or I can expect to inspire
no tenderness, no interest in those we leave
behind."

Steventon was quitted in May, with or without
deep regret, one does not know. Arrived at Bath
the Austens spent some months with the Perrotts
at their house in Paragon, during which there was
a diligent search for a suitable home.   No. 4
Sydney Place – a substantial Georgian house,
facing Sydney Gardens – was finally chosen, and
the Austens moved into it during the summer.
But, soon after, they paid a visit to Sidmouth, for
Mr. Austen, no longer tied by his clerical duties,
was free to travel so far as his circumstances permitted.   Thus in the following year they went to
Dawlish and Teignmouth, and in 1804 to Lyme
Regis.   On these occasions, Jane not only experienced staying at a seaside watering-place, but
viewed a different sort of landscape from what
hitherto she had been accustomed to.   It is doubtful if she crossed Dartmoor, but the proximity of
the Moor, the red cliffs of Sidmouth and Dawlish,

the bluer sea of South Devon, must have made their impression on one who had so sensitive an eye for the more homely aspect of the familiar Hampshire and Kent. These expeditions meant a good deal to Jane's limited experience.

Possibly travel in its larger sense might not have appealed to her. She loved nature, and in her reticent manner depicted it faithfully, but always in the manner of a neat little water-colour. She is at her best in this direction when describing a family estate, a garden, or artfully timbered park. It is likely that she would have echoed the eighteenth-century notion that a mountain was " horrid," and nature in the raw was too savage and untamed to excite admiration. She preferred the pastorals described by Thomson and Cowper, and probably was unmoved by the rhapsodies of the Romantics over crags and mountains. Moreover she was essentially a stay-at-home. In certain directions she was totally without curiosity, and one does not even feel that foreign travel was thrust from her mind simply because it was out of reach. The idea did not interest her. It was not so much patriotism, but a serene contentment, and a satisfaction with her native country which prompted her to write to a friend : " I hope your letters from abroad are satisfactory. They would not be satisfactory to *me*, I confess, unless they breathed a strong spirit of regret for not being in England." She had no shame in having a provincial, even a parochial, outlook. She was fully satisfied.

But, apart from change of environment, one of these visits to Devonshire brought Jane an experience deeper and more moving than any she had known hitherto, or was to know in future. Then for the first, and, it seems, only time in her life, she fell in love.[1]

It is a shadowy romance ; the place particularised no more definitely than Devonshire ; even the year is uncertain. The fullest details are given by Miss Lefroy, and these were based on the information of Caroline Austen, daughter of James Austen, Jane's brother.

From this it appears that, when travelling in the West of England, the Austens made the acquaintance of a Mr. Blackall, a clergyman, and that he and Jane were mutually attracted. Probably the acquaintanceship was brief. There seems to have been no definite declaration, and they parted with the suggestion either that he

[1] The incident, recounted by Sir Francis Hastings Doyle in his *Reminiscences and Opinions*, published in 1886, of Jane, in the year 1802, meeting in Switzerland a young Naval officer who became attached to her, and then promptly overtaxed his strength mountaineering and died of brain-fever, may be dismissed. There is no scrap of evidence that Jane ever left England, and the story appears to be an unaccountable fabrication, as Sir Francis himself half suggests.

should visit the Austens, or that they would meet the following summer, " implying or, perhaps, saying that he should be there also, wherever it might be." Shortly after came a letter from his brother stating that Mr. Blackall was dead.

That is all. One may read into the episode as much or as little of significance as one chooses. But it seems likely that, during this encounter, Jane was stirred profoundly, that this was a unique occasion when she was fired with a love that exceeded friendship, and that this experience, with its hope and passion, so swiftly ended, brought an added depth to her nature and a fuller under-standing of the human heart. Her love was frustrated and unfulfilled. It may not even have been avowed. Possibly it was a secret shared only with Cassandra. (And if that were the case it would strengthen still more the bond between them ; for Cassandra had suffered in similar fashion.) But whatever exactly were the par-ticulars of this hazily seen romance, it seems cer-tain that Jane suffered, and that for the remainder of her life the memory of it was fresh in her mind ; and, perhaps, now and then for a moment or two, she would indulge in self-pity. But only for a moment. And one may believe that she spoke honestly when she wrote to her niece concerning the state of mind of a rejected lover : " but it is

no creed of mine, as you must be well aware,
that such sort of disappointments kill anybody."
But that was several years later, and it is possible
that she expressed her own conviction when she
described Anne Elliot as loving longest when hope
is gone.

Certainly she was not embittered by this stroke
of fate, or by the fact that she did not marry.
She was, indeed, the perfect spinster, though here
and there one may detect a somewhat self-
conscious repudiation of spinsterhood, such as in
a letter to Fanny written in 1816 : " Single
women have a dreadful propensity for being
poor, which is one very strong argument in favour
of matrimony." But that was rare. To the end
she retained, if not the spirit of youth, a complete
understanding of youth in others. Life, what it
had given and what it had withheld, all that she
had observed and learnt of human nature, did
not sour or harden her. The cruellest shafts of
her irony are feathered with bright streamers of
humour. Very seldom did she intend to wound
deeply. Nothing could be further from fact than
to consider Jane as the traditional spinster, acid,
disillusioned, and frustrated. But it must be
remembered that she was only forty-two years of
age when she died.

There is one other sentimental episode which

must be mentioned – inconclusive and odd, show-
ing Jane for once in a mood of indecision.   This
occurred in November 1802, when Cassandra
and Jane came to stay with their brother at
Steventon, whence they went to pay a visit to
friends in the neighbourhood.   A few days later,
they reappeared unexpectedly at the Rectory, and
Jane, in a state of considerable agitation, declared
that they must at once return to Bath.   On being
questioned, she said that she had accepted an
offer of marriage, and bitterly repented her action.
The matter must be set right.   One cannot tell
whether this had taken place at Bath, or during
their absence from Steventon (in which case
Jane's would-be husband was probably Mr. Bigg-
Wither, of Manydown Park, who is said to have
proposed to her), but whoever the unfortunate
man may have been, Jane was so disturbed concerning her rash acceptance that nothing would
deter her from her determination, and James – at
some inconvenience, for the day was a Saturday
and he had no time to arrange for anyone to take
duty on Sunday – had perforce to accompany
his sisters to Bath.   Where, one supposes, she
immediately indicated her change of mind.

If, as is probable, this episode took place shortly
after the death of Mr. Blackall, Jane's vacillation
shows that she was less calm, more a servant of her

nerves, than was usual with her. That stricken, and for the moment hopeless, she snatched, without consideration, at what might well be the last opportunity of matrimony, and then, either becoming self-consciously aware that marriage of this kind would be a disloyalty to the man whom she had genuinely loved, or simply because her innate integrity would not allow her to make a marriage of convenience, suffered a complete reversal of mood. Possibly Cassandra influenced her.

At the time, the incident perturbed Jane. She would despise herself for betraying such indecision, and, hating drama in her own life, she would regret her impetuosity, and the dismay and pain it may have caused. But it is doubtful if the affair had any lasting influence on her. If it was ever alluded to, it is likely it would be in the spirit of a family joke in which, later, the possibility of her marriage to the Rector of Chawton was discussed. Just as was Jane's supposed infatuation for the poet, Crabbe, which appears to have been a source of amusement for a long time. Mrs. Austen alludes to it in a letter to a niece : " Aunt Jane desires me to tell you with her love that she has heard bad news lately, namely, that Mr. Crabbe is going to be married." While, iong after, Jane, hearing of Mrs. Crabbe's death,

FA

writes : " No : I have never seen the death of Mrs.
Crabbe. . . . It is almost ridiculous.   Poor
woman !   I will comfort *him* as well as I can, but
I do not undertake to be good to her children.
She had better not leave any."

There exist few of Jane's letters during the years
which she lived at Bath, and we have practically
no information as to her life there.   One event of
importance was the completion in first draft of
Northanger Abbey, and its sale, for the sum of ten
pounds, to the publishers, Crosbie & Co. of London,
under the title of " Susan," which implies that
Catherine Morland was originally Susan Morland.   It was, however, to prove an unfruitful
transaction, for though the book was announced
for publication it did not appear.   Possibly the
disappointment at Crosbie's obvious repentance
of the bargain, and his obduracy in refusing to
publish, may well have so disheartened Jane that
she determined to abandon authorship.   Or possibly her silence was due, as has been suggested,
to her state of mind following the death of Mr.
Blackall.   But, whatever the cause, the fact
remains that from the completion of *Northanger
Abbey* in 1803 she wrote nothing for nine years
except the uncompleted novel now known as
The Watsons.

This, from the evidence of the watermarks on

the manuscript, which bear the dates 1803 and 1804, was probably written during the latter portion of the Austens' residence at Bath. It was first published by Mr. J. E. Austen Leigh, the author of the *Memoir*, and, as recently as 1928, appeared " *The Watsons*, by Jane Austen. Completed in accordance with her instructions by Edith (her great grand-niece) and Francis Brown."

Various reasons for the non-completion of the book have been put forward. Mr. Austen Leigh says : " My own idea is, but it is only a guess, that the author became aware of the evil of having placed her heroine too low, in such a position of poverty and obscurity as, though not necessarily connected with vulgarity, has a sad tendency to degenerate into it ; and therefore, like a singer who has begun on too low a note, she discontinued the strain." This seems somewhat far-fetched. Jane, in her novels, often describes or implies arrogance and snobbery, but it was usually objectively. More reasonable is the late Mr. A. B. Walkley's idea, that the relations between the heroine Emma and Lady Osborne, and the promised duel of wits between them, bore too much resemblance to the already exploited relationship of Elizabeth and Lady Catherine de Bourgh, and that Jane, fearing repetition, laid

aside the story. It is more likely that – either for
the reasons suggested, or for others unknown – the
impulse for creation suddenly flagged. That, in a
period of disillusion, the whole business of fiction
was felt to be without interest or purpose ; and
if not definitely renounced, the habit of composition was allowed to lie dormant, until, without the
spur of ambition or acclaim, it became too great
an effort to start afresh. It was only when Jane
was nearer the climacteric, and, perhaps, in
need of some mode of activity which would permit
expression both of her thoughts of vanished youth
and the scarcely reached wisdom of middle age,
that she was once more impelled to write, and
seek comfort in fashioning for herself a world of
her imagination. But the motive would be unconscious. It would not be a deliberate way of
escape. What is called the artistic temperament
was not hers.

In the autumn of 1804, shortly after Jane had
learnt of the death, as the result of a riding accident, of her great friend, Mrs. Lefroy – and this
sorrow may have contributed to her failing interest in *The Watsons* – the Austens left their
house in Sydney Place and moved to Green Park
Buildings.

A few months later, in the January of 1805,
Mr. Austen was taken ill, and died within two

days. Though he had been in failing health for
some years the end was unexpected. Jane, writing on the day of his death to her brother, Francis,
now a Captain stationed at Dungeness, says : " I
have melancholy news to relate, & sincerely feel
for your feelings under the shock of it. – I wish
I could prepare you better for it. But having said
so much, your mind will already forstall the sort
of event which I have to communicate. – Our
dear Father has closed his virtuous & happy life,
in a death almost as free from suffering as his
Children could have wished."

   The following day, Jane writes again, for meanwhile she had learnt that Francis had moved to
Portsmouth and would thus miss her first letter.
Again she speaks of the peacefulness of Mr.
Austen's death. " To have seen him languishing
long, struggling for Hours, would have been
dreadful ! & thank God ! we were all spared from
it. Except the restlessness of high Fever, he did
not suffer – & he was mercifully spared from
knowing that he was about to quit the Objects
so beloved, so fondly cherished as his wife &
Children ever were. – His tenderness as a Father,
who can do justice to ? – My Mother is tolerably
well ; she bears up with great fortitude, but I
fear her health must suffer under such a shock. –
An express was sent for James, & he arrived here

this morning before eight o'clock. – The funeral is to be on Saturday, at Walcot Church. – The Serenity of the Corpse is most delightful ! It preserves the sweet, benevolent smile which always distinguished him."

If, to modern ears, the phrases seem a little odd and stilted they show the affection which Jane had for her parents. Her grief was deep. So was her faith. Religion for her, as with all the Austens, was assured. Hers was not the easy-going religion so widespread in the eighteenth century, which accepted God as the King was accepted ; the one ruling in Heaven, to whom prayers were said, the other in Kensington, to whom taxes were paid. There was nothing in her nature of the mystic, and little of the philosopher, but she was a convinced Christian, who must surely, with those powers of searching criticism which were hers, have subjected her creed to the test of her reason.

A few months after Mr. Austen's death, the Austens moved from their house in Green Park Buildings to lodgings in Gay Street. With the loss of the stipends of Deane and Steventon, Mrs. Austen was impoverished, and the income of herself and her daughters did not amount to more than £240 a year, which included the income from the £1,000 bequeathed to

Cassandra by Thomas Fowle. Mrs. Austen's sons,
however, contributed to her maintenance. Francis
was particularly generous, but Mrs. Austen
would only accept half the sum that he offered.
Enough income, however, was at her disposal
for her to live in comfort for the remainder of
her life, and there is never any complaint of
poverty.

During the summer of 1806, Mrs. Austen took
Jane on a visit to her relative, the Reverend
Thomas Leigh, who had recently inherited
Stoneleigh Abbey in Warwickshire. In a letter
to a daughter-in-law, Mrs. Austen recounts, with
a good deal of gusto, the beauties and luxuries
of the Abbey. " We found ourselves," she says,
" on Tuesday eating fish, venison, and all manner
of good things, in a large and noble parlour,
hung round with family portraits. The house is
larger than I could have supposed. We cannot
find our way about it. . . . In the morning we
say our prayers in a handsome chapel. Then
follows breakfast, consisting of chocolate, coffee,
and tea, plum cake, pound cake, hot rolls,
cold rolls, bread and butter, and dry toast for me.
The house steward, a fine, large, respectable-
looking man, orders all these matters." Mrs.
Austen's admiration and astonishment are further
excited by the quantity of fruit which " exceeds

anything you can form any idea of, the fish ponds, the park, the dairy, the forty-five windows in the front of the house, and the number of casks of strong-beer in the cellar which is beyond imagination." And the fact that everything is "kept so clean, that were you to cut your finger I do not think you could find a cobweb to wrap it in."

Mrs. Austen was a woman of character, humour, and vigour, though, from Jane's frequent references to her mother's complainings, she was something of a *malade imaginaire*. But only a half-hearted one, for she could write the following verses, which date from the first years of her residence at Bath, and are an amusing tribute to her doctor, Bowen.

DIALOGUE BETWEEN DEATH AND MRS. A.

Says Death, " I've been trying these four weeks and
   more
To seize an old Madam here at Number Four,
Yet I still try in vain, th' she's turned of three score ;
To what is my ill-success owing ? "

" I'll tell you old Felloe if you cannot guess
To what you're indebted for your ill success —
To the prayers of my husband, whose love I possess,

To the care of my daughters, whom Heaven will bless,
To the skill and attention of Bowen."

By the end of 1806 the Austens had moved to
Southampton. The choice of this town was
influenced by the fact that they could share a
house with Francis and his wife. He had recently
married, and was on shore until the April of the
following year. His wife was a Mary Gibson,
and there was some disappointment in the Austen
family that the attachment which he evidently
had for Martha Lloyd – daughter of Mrs. Lloyd,
of Ibthorpe, and sister of Mary Lloyd who was
now Mrs. James Austen – did not at this time
materialise. It was long after Jane's death, and,
for Mary, many years of waiting, that he made
her his second wife.

During the Peace of Amiens, in 1802, Francis
had been put on half-pay, but when war was
renewed, little more than twelve months later,
he was sent to Ramsgate to raise troops called
" Sea Fencibles." Here it was that he first met
Miss Gibson. During the blockade of Boulogne,
Francis was up and down the coast, both ashore,
and in the *Leopard*, and it appears that he found
opportunities of continuing his acquaintance
with her. Following Napoleon's final abandonment of his preparations to invade England the

blockading squadron was disbanded, and shortly after, Francis was appointed Flag-Captain in the *Canopus*, and saw a variety of service. For this ship was among those which took part in the abortive chase of Villeneuve's fleet, after its escape from Toulon in the spring of 1805, across the Atlantic and back to Spain.

Canopus was on convoy duty during the battle of Trafalgar, and Francis, writing to Mary Gibson, bemoans his luck in missing the action; an opinion which is echoed in the log of the ship, which, on the day the news of Trafalgar was received, bears the heading : " Off Gibraltar, a melancholy situation." Francis, however, shortly afterwards saw active service, for *Canopus* was once more dispatched to the West Indies, took part in the battle of St. Domingo, and helped in the capture of several prizes – a fact that must have been some compensation for the loss of the command of a frigate which Francis states he hoped, had he lived, Lord Nelson would have given him.

It has been often remarked how slight an interest Jane appears to have taken in the affairs of her day. And when one considers that during her life occurred the huge, reverberating upheaval of the French Revolution, the rise of Napoleon, the subsequent period when practically the whole of Europe became the stage for his megalomaniac activities, and England was engaged in almost ceaseless warfare, it is certainly surprising that no echo of these terrific events disturbed the peace of Steventon, Godmersham, or Chawton ; or, for that matter, the peace of Mansfield Park and Northanger Abbey. This detachment strikes one as almost inhuman. That the horrors of the Revolution, the menace of France, the bogy of Napoleon and his legions across the narrow seas – insisted upon by Hardy, who tells of villagers sleepless from fear of invasion – the triumphs of Nelson and Wellington, the whole drama of these years, should be ignored, speaks of either a stoicism or an incuriousness which requires explanation. There is no satisfactory one to be given, but by contrasting the methods of transport and communication in the days of the Georges and in modern times some understanding may be obtained.

To the generation that has experienced the Great War, during which practically the whole of the nation, if not actually engaged in some way or another on its prosecution, was influenced, by its events, it is natural to assume that the wars of a hundred years ago involved the same processes, and it seems strange that life in England could remain so undisturbed and normal. But

it must be remembered that then war was primarily a matter for professional armies and
navies ; nations were not organised for war. It
was, indeed, less of a whole-time occupation,
even for armies. It was considered normal that
wives should accompany their husbands to the
Peninsula during the campaign – to cite one
small instance of differences. A greater differ-
ence was the slowness of movement ; and still
more the slowness of receiving news. Before the
days of telephones and telegraphs – which during
the Great War could keep the whole world posted
hour by hour with the course of events – news
travelled slowly, and disaster or victory were days,
if not weeks, in the past by the time dispatches
reached London. During the long intervals
between decisions, either of policy or of battle,
interest must inevitably have waned. There was
no keying up of expectancy ; seldom any pre-
paration for astonishment. Moreover, the sense
of distance must have been much greater. To
the majority, the battle of the Nile or the retreat
from Moscow, might have been affairs enacted
upon another planet.

Yet, granting all these differences and changes,
it strikes one as curious that Jane, in her novels,
makes scarcely any reference to the European
scene, certainly does not seek assistance from it

for the purposes of plot, or even remark its influence upon character. And the reader, suddenly considering this, is surprised that the serene life which Jane describes, with its unanxious women, its untroubled young men, attending to their estates, doing business or doing nothing, was contemporary with the prolonged tension of the Napoleonic wars.

Against this charge it may be urged that Jane kept rigorously to the life which was immediately under her observation, and in these matters, as in others outside her experience, she was determined not to adventure. And even on the world which she knew, she imposed limitations. With her we do not enter either a cottage or a palace ; the life of the peasantry is not touched upon. A bedroom must contain an invalid before we are allowed entrance. The taboos are numerous. And when this is realised, one begins to understand that deliberately and continuously she worked within her self-imposed limits. That she surrounded the world of her fiction with a definite boundary – as exclusive as a ring-fence surrounding one of her gentlemen's parks – and never explored, even if she had wished to do so, beyond it.

This being appreciated, it is a little easier to understand her avoidance of references to current

affairs, however insistent – at least to our eyes –
they must have been.

Essentially, too, she was a woman whose nerves
were well under control, and even her imagination, penetrating as it was. It was not in her
nature, to endure fears of possible evil, or to
suffer from regrets. When the moment for sorrow
came, she felt intensely ; but she did not antici-
pate it. She lived very much in the moment, as
her absorption in detail testifies. Hers was a disposition which precluded not only imaginative
anxiety, or even speculation, regarding the devel-
opment of vast events, but anxiety as to the fate
of her brothers, in spite of her manifest love for
them. Her agitations were reserved for small
occasions, for tremendous trifles, passionately felt,
but swiftly forgotten. Certainly she did not brood
over disaster and terror. " How horrible it is to
have so many killed !" she writes in 1811. "And
what a blessing that one cares for none of them ! "
That is all. Both exclamations are, one feels, sincere, but the emotions which prompted them are
fleeting. In many ways she was like a child in-
tent upon the thing immediately before its eyes,
and only fully employing imagination for imaginary or semi-imaginary things.

The house taken by the Austens at Southampton was in Castle Square. Mr. J. E. Austen

Leigh, the author of the *Memoir*, who at the time
of Jane's residence there was a boy of about ten,
describes it fully. " My grandmother's house,"
he writes, " had a pleasant garden, bounded on
one side by the old city walls ; the top of this
wall was sufficiently wide to afford a pleasant
walk, easily accessible to ladies by steps. . . . At
that time Castle Square was occupied by a fan-
tastic edifice, too large for the space on which it
stood, though too small to accord well with its
castellated style, erected by the second Marquis
of Lansdowne, half-brother to the well-known
statesman, who succeeded him in the title. The
Marchioness had a light phaeton, drawn by six,
and sometimes by eight little ponies, each pair
decreasing in size, and becoming lighter in colour,
through all the shades of dark brown, light brown,
bay and chestnut. . . . It was a delight to me
to look down from the window and see this fairy
equipage put together ; for the premises of this
castle were so contracted that the whole process
went on in the little space that remained of the
open square. Like other fairy works, however,
it all proved evanescent. Not only carriage and
ponies, but castle itself, soon vanished away. . . .
On the death of the Marquis in 1809, the castle
was pulled down. Few probably remember its
existence ; and any one who might visit the place

now would wonder how it ever could have stood there."

To-day, the house inhabited by the Austens has met the same fate as the Castle, and there is no trace either of it or the garden which was " considered the best in the town." Jane refers to it with some detail in a letter written soon after the move to Southampton. " Our Garden is putting in order, by a Man who bears a remarkably good character, has a very fine complexion & asks something less than the first. The shrubs which border the gravel walk he says are only sweetbriar & roses, & the latter of an indifferent sort ; — we mean to get a few of a better kind therefore, & at my own particular desire he procures us some Syringas. I could not do without a Syringa, for the sake of Cowper's line. – We talk also of a Laburnam. – The Border under the Terrace Wall, is clearing away to receive Currant & Gooseberry Bushes, & a spot is found very proper for raspberries." She writes in somewhat similar strain from Chawton, and evidently Jane was something of a gardener. She, of course, knew nothing of the herbaceous borders and Alpines from which the modern gardener derives so much consolation, and she was immune from the fever for horticulture so pleasantly prevalent to-day, but in her manner she took keen interest and pleasure in the flowers and fruits of Mrs. Austen's gardens, which, at all events partially, were under her direction.

Life at Southampton was agreeable enough. Neighbours called. Indeed, Jane complains, " Our acquaintance increase too fast." Frank, on leave, has some skating. Relatives pay visits, and are taken for excursions. There are balls at the Assembly Rooms, after one of which, Jane comments : " The room was tolerably full, & there were perhaps thirty couple of Dancers – the melancholy part was, to see so many dozen young Women standing by without partners, & each of them with two ugly naked shoulders ! – It was the same room in which we danced 15 years ago ! – I thought it all over – & in spite of the shame of being so much older, felt with thankfulness that I was quite as happy now as then." This was true. Her life in its narrow orbit was a full one, though its occupations were, for a woman of her nature and her superb talent, trivial. Certainly she did not during this time employ that talent, and the only reference to literary work during the years she spent at Southampton is a letter, a copy of which, in her handwriting, was preserved by Cassandra, to the publishers, Crosbie & Co. It requests that a reply should be directed to Mrs. Ashton Dennis,

G A

Post Office, Southampton, was signed A. D., and enquires concerning a MS. novel sold in the year 1803 for the sum of £10. The letter concludes : " Six years have since passed, and this work, of which I am myself the Authoress, has never to my knowledge appeared in print, tho' an early publication was stipulated for at the time of sale." To which the publisher replied that there had been no stipulation and that he was under no obligation to publish.

In June of 1808, Jane paid another visit to Godmersham, whence she writes at length of brothers, sisters-in-law, nephews, and nieces, and a multitude of friends. Of eating strawberries, of writing in the Yellow Room, journeying to Canterbury, playing at Commerce or Spillikins – at which now almost forgotten diversion she was an adept – and also at cup-and-ball. At cup-and-ball her proficiency is stated to have been "marvellous. She has been known to catch the ball on the point above a hundred times in succession."

In these and other letters written from Godmersham, the reader has the impression of a country-life, easy, gracious, and not without dignity. Edward managing his estates with scrupulous care and attention, his wife managing her household with equal competence, and bringing up her children – among whom was Fanny, so

dear to Jane – with a judicious affection. Its
happy tenor was, however, soon to be broken.
Little more than three months after Jane's return
to Southampton, Mrs. Knight died in child-birth.
Jane, in a letter to Cassandra, who was at Godmersham, writes of the event with evident
emotion : " We have felt, we do feel, for you all –
as you will not need to be told – for you, for Fanny,
for Henry, for Lady Brydges, & for dearest
Edward, whose loss and whose sufferings seem to
make those of evry other person nothing. – God
be praised ! that you can say what you do of him
– that he has a religious Mind to bear him up, &
a Disposition that will gradually lead him to comfort. My dear, dear Fanny ! – I am so thankful
that she has you with her ! – You will do everything for her, you will give her all the Consolation
that human aid can give. – May the Almighty
sustain you all." Two days later Jane writes
again : " Edward's loss is terrible, and must be
felt as such, and these are too early days indeed
to think of moderation in grief, either in him or
his afflicted daughter, but soon we may hope that
our dear Fanny's sense of duty to that beloved
father will rouse her to exertion. For his sake,
and as the most acceptable proof of love to the
spirit of her departed mother, she will try to be
tranquil and resigned. . . . Your account of

Lizzie is very interesting. Poor child ! One must hope the impression *will* be strong, and yet one's heart aches for a dejected mind of eight years old."

Jane showed her sorrow in a practical manner, for when, ten days after Mrs. Knight's death, two of her sons came from Steventon to Southampton, she shows a very charming sympathy and understanding of the boys' mood. She concurs when buying them mourning, when they " find that black pantaloons are considered by them as necessary, and of course one would not have them uncomfortable by the want of what is usual on such occasions." She walks with them, takes them for a little water-party to Northam, plays various games, accompanies them to church on Sunday, and, in the evening, gives a reading of " the Psalms and Lessons, and a sermon at home, to which they were very attentive ; but you will not expect to hear that they did not return to conundrums the moment it *was over*."

The letter to Cassandra which describes the boys' visit brightly illuminates that side of Jane's character which was so attractive to children and young people, and makes one comprehend the love, rather that of a contemporary than of an elder, which her nephews and nieces had for her. She had the art of being serious when seriousness was wished for ; of sharing problems

and difficulties which, one imagines, she discussed
in a manner that forbade the least suspicion of
patronage or adult advice, so that confessor and
confidante were equal. While on frivolous occasions she had so genuine an interest in amusements
and games that it increased the zest of the players.
Then she provided an almost rollicking idea of
fun, and at any moment would embark on flights
of nonsense or of fancy, which would fill her list-
eners with expectation and surprise. Jane was,
without doubt, not only an adored, but an ador-
able, aunt.

Not long after the death of his wife, Edward
Knight suggested to Mrs. Austen that she should
move from Southampton, and put either of two
houses at her disposal. The one in Kent, the
other on his Chawton estate in Hampshire.
Francis now being on foreign service in the East,
and his wife free to live where she chose, the
decision to leave Southampton was taken, and
Chawton fixed upon. The move was made in
1809, and by the summer of that year, Mrs.
Austen, Cassandra, Jane, and Mary Lloyd –
sister of James Austen's second wife, who at that
time lived with them – were installed at Chawton
Cottage, whence Jane, on the 26th July, wrote a
rhyming letter to Francis, congratulating him on
the birth of a son. The letter concludes :

As for ourselves, we're very well ;
As unaffected prose will tell. –
Cassandra's pen will paint our state,
The many comforts that await
Our Chawton home, how much we find
Already in it, to our mind ;
And how convinced, that when complete
It will all other Houses beat
That ever has been made or mended,
With rooms concise, or rooms distended.

CHAPTER IV

1809–1816

THE village of Chawton lies about a mile from the small market-town of Alton in Hampshire. Chawton Cottage is a house of mellow red brick, standing at a point where the road forks to Portsmouth and Winchester. It is built directly on the road, and any passer-by could have looked through the window as easily as the family friend who reported that, when driving past in a post-chaise, he had seen the Austens "looking very comfortable at breakfast."

Recently a tablet has been placed on the wall of the cottage, stating that "Jane Austen lived here from 1809–1817 and hence all her works went into the world." A visitor may obtain admission, but the privilege is disappointing. A portion of the house is now the premises of a village club, and the remainder is divided between two tenants. The room most associated with Jane retains a simple Georgian mantelpiece, with carved medallions and swags, but the contemporary grate has been removed, and the present furnishing is destructive of any attempt to picture the room as it was when Jane was writing there. So it is with the rest of the house. The exterior, however, remains substantially unchanged since the Austens' day. One can see traces of the large window of the drawing-room Mrs. Austen had blocked up, and the new window, thrown out at her direction, which looked into the garden – at that time screened from the Winchester road by a high wooden fence. This has now vanished, and also a small pond. The garden was of a fair extent, and Jane took an eager interest in it. More than once she refers to flowers and fruits making their appearance, and in a letter written two years after settling at Chawton : " You cannot imagine – it is not in Human Nature to imagine – what a nice walk we have round the Orchard. The row of Beech look very well indeed, & so does the young Quickset hedge in the Garden " – which implies that a good deal of planting and improving was done when the Austens first moved to Chawton. Nothing now remains of the shrubbery and gravel-walks which are described, but there are some fully grown elms and yews which must certainly have shaded Jane in her perambulations, and an oak-tree that, it is said, she planted herself.

Chawton House, at that time in the ownership of Edward Knight, is situated only a few hundred

yards from the cottage. Its grey façade may be
seen from the Portsmouth road, on the further
side of a shallow valley, in the cup of which
is Chawton Church – rebuilt after a fire that
occurred in 1843. It contains, however, several
memorials to the Knights, and there are tablets
to both the elder and younger Cassandra, while
in the churchyard are their graves. Chawton
House is a beautiful example of an early sixteenth-
century manor, with many mullioned windows
looking over the park and gardens. Within is
much fine panelling and a sequence of family
portraits.

Edward Knight lived for the most part at Godmersham, but he stayed at Chawton each year,
often for a considerable time, when there was a
constant interchange of visits between the Great
House – as it was called – and the cottage. Apart
from this association, Mrs. Austen frequently had
various members of the increasing number of
grandchildren with her ; Steventon was not
distant, and there were friends in the neighbourhood, though with none of them does Jane appear
to have had any intimacy. For the most part she
lived an even more retired life than she had done
hitherto. She and Cassandra – two years her
elder – were drifting easily and pleasantly towards
middle life. Now she always wore a cap.

Caroline Austen, youngest daughter of James, has written vivid recollections concerning her aunt's life at Chawton, but, as she was only a girl of twelve at Jane's death, presumably much of the detail must have been hearsay – probably recounted by the ever-faithful and loving Cassandra. She mentions, once more, her needlework, and remarks that at this time Jane played the piano regularly, practising each morning, usually before a nine-o'clock breakfast, mostly from manuscript music written out by herself. Several months before the move to Chawton, Jane had anticipated this, for she wrote to her sister : " Yes, yes, we *will* have a pianoforte, and I will practise country dances, that we may have some amusement for our nephews and nieces, when we have the pleasure of their company." For the rest there were household duties, shared with Cassandra (Mrs. Austen, in spite of her vitality, having relinquished housekeeping), the writing of innumerable letters, walking, and the reading of books obtained from the circulating library at Alton.

Jane was a somewhat indiscriminate reader, without any particular enthusiasms. Of novelists, her favourites were Richardson, Fanny Burney, and Maria Edgeworth. Of *Waverley* she writes : " Walter Scott has no business to

write novels, especially good ones. – It is not
fair. – He has Fame and Profit enough as a Poet,
and should not take the bread out of other
people's mouths. – I do not like him, & do not
mean to like Waverley if I can help it – but fear
I must." *Marmion* she did not care for. She recounts having read *The Corsair*, but makes no
comment upon it. Neither does she on Boswell's
Tour of the Hebrides, and the *Life of Johnson*. The
names of many books, both fiction and otherwise,
occur in Jane's letters, but usually they are mentioned without criticism. Cowper, of contemporary poets, was most admired by her, though
she was familiar with many others, if one may
judge from the remarks made by Sir Edward
Denham, a character in Jane's unfinished novel,
Sanditon, who declares : " If ever there was a Man
who *felt*, it was Burns. – Montgomery has all the
Fire of Poetry, Wordsworth has the true soul of it.
Campbell in his Pleasures of Hope has touched the
extreme of our sensations. – If Scott *has* a fault it
is the want of Passion. Tender, Elegant Descriptions, but *Tame*."

How soon after arrival at Chawton, Jane once
more turned to her literary work is not known.
But by the spring of 1811, Jane had not only
given the manuscript of *Sense and Sensibility*
another revision – possibly she re-wrote the

greater part of it – but publication had been arranged, for she writes : " No indeed, I am never too busy to think of *S & S*.   I can no more forget it, than a mother can forget her sucking child ; & I am much obliged to you for your enquiries.   I have had two sheets to correct. . . ."

The book was published, on commission, by T. Egerton of the Military Library, Whitehall, and was a closely guarded secret, for, shortly before publication, Cassandra begs a correspondent not to " mention that Aunt Jane wrote *Sense and Sensibility*."   It appeared in October, and was advertised in *The Morning Chronicle*, first, as " A novel called *Sense and Sensibility* by Lady ——," next, as " An extraordinary novel by Lady ——," and finally, more coolly, as " An interesting novel.   Author, Lady A."

There are no records either of the negotiations regarding publication, or of the manner in which the book was received by the public.   And we have no account of Jane's natural excitement when she received copies of the three volumes, price 15*s.*, in which the book was published, and, after many years of waiting, saw her work in print.   But that it was from the start a reasonable success may be gathered from the fact that every copy was sold, that Jane received the sum of £140 (which she calls a " prodigious

recompense for that which has cost me nothing "),
and that at the end of two years a second edition
was called for. Meanwhile, Egerton had bought
Pride and Prejudice, for £110, and published it.
This was in January 1813 ; and, more important,
Jane had before this begun the writing of a completely new novel, destined to be *Mansfield Park*.

Her methods of work have been described. She
had no private study, and her desk was in the
general sitting-room. Here she wrote on small
pieces of paper, which were easily hidden when
visitors or servants interrupted her, for no one
except her immediate family was to know of her
occupation. Indeed her reticence was so great
she -insisted that the creak of the door, which
led out of the room, should not be remedied, as
it afforded her a warning of anyone's approach.
This secrecy regarding her composition was maintained long after the fact of her authorship was
acknowledged ; which was done a few months
following the publication of *Pride and Prejudice*. A
good many relatives and friends must have had
shrewd suspicions regarding Jane's published
books, but by September her authorship had been
definitely disclosed, not altogether with Jane's
approval. She appears to have been in two
minds as to whether she desired anonymity or
not, for she writes to her brother, Francis, then

with the Baltic Fleet : " Henry heard *P. & P.*
warmly praised in Scotland, by Lady Robt Kerr
& another Lady ; – & what does he do in the
warmth of his Brotherly vanity & Love, but
immediately tell them who wrote it ! A Thing
once set going in that way one knows how it
spreads ! – and he, dear Creature, has set it
going so much more than once. I know it is all
done from affection & partiality – but at the same
time, let me again express to you & Mary my
sense of the *superior* kindness which you have
shewn on the occasion, in doing what I wished. –
I am trying to harden myself. After all, what a
trifle it is in all its Bearings, to the really important
points of one's existence even in this World ! "

Jane had a genuine diffidence, and it was
natural that she should shrink from any sort of
publicity, not, perhaps, so much on her own
account but on that of her work. She would
dread ridicule or harsh criticism of a book which
she refers to as " my own darling child." With
a certain squeamishness, which was in her nature
where she herself was concerned, she might regard
publication as almost an illegitimate parenthood,
and, though not denying it – probably at heart
she would be proud of it – she would resent
criticism of her offspring. This is indicated by
her delight in Cassandra's praise, in that of her

young niece, Fanny Knight, and, presently, that
of Warren Hastings.

She makes frequent references to *Pride and
Prejudice* in her letters to Cassandra. More than
once she suffered what she terms " fits of disgust "
in regard to it. She feels it is " rather too light,
and bright, and sparkling ; it wants shade." But
on the whole she was satisfied, particularly with
the character of Elizabeth, who was the favourite
among her heroines ; as she has been with count-
less readers. Elizabeth for her was a vivid and
almost real personality, and it was not, one feels,
an exaggerated pretence that when, a few months
after the publication of her adventures, Jane,
visiting an exhibition of pictures in Spring
Gardens, said that she had seen a portrait of Mrs.
Bingley " excessively like her," but could find
none of Elizabeth Darcy. " I can only imagine,"
she says, " that Mr. D. prizes any Picture of her
too much to like it should be exposed to the public
eye. – I can imagine he w^d have that sort of feeling – that mixture of Love, Pride & Delicacy."
She had that same " mixture " regarding her
work.

In the spring of 1813, Mr. Henry Austen's wife
(once Elizabeth de Feuillade) died. Jane stayed
with her brother, in Sloane Street, shortly after,
and, writing of his state of health, throws a

discriminating light on his character. " Upon
the whole his Spirits are very much recovered. – If
I may so express myself, his Mind is not a Mind
for affliction. He is too Busy, too active, too san-
guine. – Sincerely as he was attached to poor
Eliza moreover, & excellently as he behaved to
her, he was always so used to be away from her
at times, that her Loss is not felt as that of many
a young wife might be, especially when all the
circumstances of her long and dreadful Illness
are taken into the account. – He very long knew
that she must die, & indeed it was a release at
last."

One feels that here Jane was really endeavour-
ing to refute a charge of heartlessness. It was not
in her nature to brood, and she, understanding
the elasticity of Henry's character more clearly
than others may have done, wished to explain
any apparent callousness in his attitude. In
disaster or sorrow, her imagination, as always,
was well under control. She would never indulge
in exaggeration, either of grief or of happiness,
and she believed that Henry, with whom she was
greatly in sympathy, was like her. His mind,
and hers, was, as she says, " not a Mind for
affliction." Any abandonment to sorrow was too
near akin to the passionate emotions she never
fully comprehended.

In her frequent visits to London – usually *en route* to Kent – Jane attended theatres, exhibitions, concerts, churches, drove in the parks, shopped, witnessed the performances of Indian jugglers. But though her interest in these things was observant and lively, as she states herself, " my preference for Men & Women, always inclines me to attend more to the company than the sight." An exception may be made to the shopping. Jane was an ardent shopper, and retails, with evident delight, her purchases, particularly if they were bargains. She had a pleasant vanity, and one fancies that her dress was not only of an exceptional neatness, but had an individual taste, though she was a follower of fashion, and is careful to note its changes. Of jewellery she possessed little. The topaz cross and gold chain given to her by Charles – bought from the prize money received after the capture of the privateer *La Furie* – are mentioned by her as something exceptional.

Her liking for music was a tempered one. It never lent her wings. Describing a party at Sloane Street, she says : " The Drawing room being soon hotter than we liked, we placed ourselves in the connecting Passage, which was comparatively cool, & gave us all the advantage of the Music at a pleasant distance, as well as that of the first view of every new comer. – I was quite

Ha

surrounded by acquaintance, especially Gentlemen." The new-comers and the Gentlemen were,
one feels, more enthralling than the songs, " The
Red Cross Knight " and " Poor Insect," and the
harp and pianoforte duets which formed part of
the programme. At a later date she writes, with
a sense almost of shock : " I have been listening
to dreadful Insanity. – It is Mr. Haden's firm
belief that a person *not* musical is fit for every sort
of Wickedness. I ventured to assert a little on the
other side, but I wished the cause in abler hands."

Jane's appreciation of the drama was deeper,
but qualified. She says : " Acting seldom satis-
fies me. I think I want something more than
can be." She frequently went to the theatre
when in London, and gives some account to
Cassandra of the plays which she saw. She expresses enthusiasm for the acting of Edmund
Kean. But though she took an evident pleasure
in the sights and activity of London, she must
always have returned to the country with relief.
Her most vital interests were concentrated on her
family, friends, and acquaintances, for whose
doings she had an insatiable curiosity and sympathy. And now, in the late thirties, she was
becoming more attracted to a tranquil rural life ;
and her writing was absorbing more and more of
her attention. It was amusing to visit dear Henry

in London, and Edward at Godmersham, but life at Chawton Cottage had its own interests. Certainly she did not find it dull. Jane was never bored. When alone, her imagination prevented boredom, and when with people, of whatever sort, she was enthralled and delighted as she watched the play and interplay of character. Alert, sensitive, she gathered that knowledge which enabled her to add a point of colour or a significant line to her famous, " little bit [two inches wide] of ivory on which I work with so fine a brush, as produces little effect after much labour."

In her walks and drives she would take note of the landscapes which are painted in her novels. Her descriptive writing is unobtrusive, and at times is dry and in the nature of a catalogue. The streets and squares of Bath are named with almost guide-book accuracy, but there is no presentation or appreciation of the dignity and beauty of the city. The animated bustle of the village street at Highbury in *Emma* is almost exceptional in its combined detail and vivacity, while the accounts of the various gardens and estates where Jane's characters so often congregate – Pemberley, Donwell Abbey, Delaford – are pictorially exact, but appear to have been written without particular feeling. But Jane in these things always avoided overstatement. "The country is very beautiful. I saw as much as ever to admire in my yesterday's journey," she writes in a letter, and usually her descriptions echo this precision and restraint. It was not until she wrote *Persuasion* that there was more colour and emotion in her landscapes, except for a passage in *Mansfield Park*, where for once she abandons her neat, decorous prose, and describes not only the visual scene but the mood which it inspired. It is worth quoting in full.

" His eyes soon turned, like hers, towards the scene without, where all that was solemn, and soothing, and lovely, appeared in the brilliancy of an unclouded night, and the contrast of the deep shade of the woods. Fanny spoke her feelings. ' Here's harmony ! ' said she ; ' here's repose ! Here's what may leave all painting and all music behind, and what poetry only can attempt to describe ! Here's what may tranquilise every care, and lift the heart to rapture ! When I look out on such a night as this, I feel as if there could be neither wickedness nor sorrow in the world ; and there certainly would be less of both if the sublimity of nature were more attended to, and people were carried more out of themselves by contemplating such a scene.' "

By March 1814, the novel from which this

passage is taken was completed, and Henry began
to read it while travelling in a post-chaise to
London. His "approbation is equal to my
wishes," Jane said. A few days later, Henry had
finished the book, and his approbation was not
lessened. By June the book was published –
again by Mr. Egerton of Whitehall – for we learn
that a certain Mr. Cooke finds it "the most
sensible novel he ever read." By November the
first edition was sold. Two years later it was
published in Paris, where *Emma* and *Sense and
Sensibility* had already appeared in 1815 and 1816,
the latter under the title of " *Raison et Sensibilité ou
les Deux Manières d'Aimer,*" *traduit librement de
L'Anglais.* As Jane makes no references to these
translations, it is possible that she was ignorant
of them, but it is interesting that one of her
works had appeared in Paris in the year of
Waterloo.

Throughout 1814, Jane was writing *Emma.*
Twice that year she stayed in London. First at
Henrietta Street, where Henry had his banking
business, and later at Hans Place, whither he
moved some time after the death of his wife. The
house had a garden, which Jane calls "quite a
love," and the surroundings were then so rural
that she speaks of "walking into London." She
seems to have been very content staying with

Henry, but she is not enthusiastic concerning a lady from Hanwell, whom he is evidently considering as a second wife, though she is convinced that he will marry again. This he did, but not for three years after her death, by which time his choice was a Miss Eleanor Jackson.

Emma was finished in the spring of 1815, but publication did not take place until the end of the year. That summer, Edward Knight spent several months at Chawton while Godmersham was being renovated, and Jane was delighted in having the companionship of Fanny, and her brothers, though there was one of whom Jane wrote with a hint of disapproval. " Edward," she says, " is no Enthusiast in the beauties of Nature. His Enthusiasm is for the sports of the field only. He is a very promising & pleasing young Man however upon the whole, behaves with great propriety to his Father & great kindness to his Brothers & Sisters & we must forgive his thinking more of Growse & Partridges than Lakes & Mountains."

It is uncertain when the manuscript of *Emma* was submitted to the famous publisher, Mr. John Murray, but by October, Jane, once more in London, says that she has received a letter from him, and goes on to remark : " He is a rogue of course, but a civil one. He offers £450 but wants to have the copyright of *M. P.* & *S. S.* included. It will end in my publishing for myself I daresay. He sends more praise however than I expected." In the same letter she mentions that Henry is not quite well, and in an addition, written on the following day, " Henry's illness is much more serious than I expected. It is a fever – something bilious but chiefly inflammatory." Henry was, in fact, dangerously ill, and Jane, for many weeks, was at Hans Place, nursing him with a devotion that impaired her own health. This illness caused delay in negotiations with Mr. Murray, for the business was in her brother's hands, and he was unable to deal with any correspondence. Finally, Jane requested Mr. Murray to call upon her, with the hope that " A short conversation may perhaps do more than much writing." Which it appears to have done, for, not long after, Jane is complaining at the delay in receiving proofs, and asks : " Is it likely that the printers will be influenced to greater dispatch and punctuality by knowing that the work is to be dedicated, by permission, to the Prince Regent ? " This naivety seems to have been effective, for, the next day, Mr. Murray is very polite, gives the blame to the stationer, who had kept the printers waiting for paper, and assures Miss Austen that there shall be no further cause for dissatisfaction.

The princely dedication had been brought
about owing to Henry being attended in his illness
by one of the Regent's physicians, who had in-
formed him that the authoress was staying in
London. Whereupon, the Regent, who was an
admirer of her work, and kept a set of her novels
" in every one of his residences," commanded
that the Rev. J. S. Clarke, his librarian,
should wait upon Jane to suggest he should,
at her convenience, conduct her over Carlton
House.

It is to be deplored that she left no record
of this visit, for Jane at Carlton House, with its
stucco and its marble, its candelabra and its
sphinxes, under the guidance of the learned Mr.
Clarke, is an amusing picture. Possibly for her
it was not so entertaining as it may seem to us
in retrospect. She might have been too " sensible of the honour," as the phrase goes – certainly
Mr. Clarke would have been – and unable at
the time to reply in speech to his pomposities
so adroitly as later she was to do in correspondence. But outwardly self-assured, inwardly a
little nervous, half fearful, half hopeful that she
would be presented to His Royal Highness himself, she must have enjoyed both the actual visit
and its implications. Her loyalty might be in

conflict with her sense of fun and of contrast, yet as she passed down the high corridors, and was shown the treasures of the library, the array of *objets d'art* in the saloons, her peculiar humour must surely have delighted in the fact that she, a neat, middle-aged spinster, daughter of a country rector, dressed in her best, was permitted to wander among the scenes of those almost fabulous Regency orgies on the introduction of, among others, Mrs. Norris, Mr. Collins, and the Dashwood family.

Two days after this visit, Jane writes to Mr. Clarke : " Among the many flattering attentions which I rec^d from you at Carlton House on Monday last, was the Information of my being at liberty to dedicate any future work to HRH the P.R. without any solicitation on my part." But she was a little doubtful of the validity of this permission, saying she would be " equally concerned to appear either Presumptuous or Ungrateful," and entreats Mr. Clarke to inform her precisely what has been intended. To which Mr. Clarke replies that permission to dedicate any book is given. Further, he expresses a hope that Jane in some future work will delineate " the Habits of Life and Character and enthusiasm of a Clergyman who should be something like Beatties Minstrel,

Silent when glad, affectionate, tho' shy
And now his look was most demurely sad
& now he laughed aloud yet none knew why –

Neither D. Goldsmith – nor La Fontaine in his
Tableau de Famille – have in my mind quite
delineated an English Clergyman, at least of the
present day – Fond of, & entirely engaged in
Literature – no man's Enemy but his own.   Pray
Madam think of these things."

A curious, if pious, wish with which Jane, quite
naturally, felt herself to be totally incapable of
complying.   " The comic part of the character
I might be equal to," she writes, " but not the
good, the enthusiastic, the literary.   Such a man's
conversation must at times be on subjects of science
and philosophy, of which I know nothing. . . .
A classical education, or at any rate a very extensive acquaintance with English literature,
ancient and modern, appears to me to be quite
indispensable for the person who would do any
justice to your clergyman ; and I think I may
boast myself to be, with all possible vanity, the
most unlearned and uninformed female who ever
dared to be an authoress."

Upon which Mr. Clarke, unctuous and syco-
phantic, replies, thanking her for " the Letter you
were so obliging as to do me the Honour of
sending," harping once more on his clergyman,

and informing her that he is to stay with Lord
Egremont, then at the Pavilion at Brighton,
before returning to London to preach on Thanks-
giving Day. He ends, almost equivocally : " Pray,
dear Madam, remember, that besides My Cell
at Carlton House, I have another which Dr.
Barne procured for me at No : 37. Golden Square –
where I often hide myself. There is a small
Library there much at your Service – and if you
can make the Cell render you any service as a
sort of Halfway House, when you come to Town –
I shall be most happy. There is a Maid Servant
of mine always there."

But one feels that Jane did not avail herself of
this. invitation.

Soon after *Emma* was published, dedicated
most respectfully to the Regent by " his dutiful
and obedient humble servant." In due course
a copy was dispatched to His Royal Highness
which Mr. Clarke suitably acknowledges, and,
after suggesting that Jane may choose to dedicate
her next novel to Prince Leopold, ends with,
not unexpected egregiousness : " Any historical
romance, illustrative of the history of the august
House of Cobourg, would just now be very
interesting."

Jane's answer is masterly in its restraint and
decorum, giving scarely a sign of the amusement

which this suggestion must have caused her ;
though perhaps Mr. Clarke did not wholly appreciate her remark in reference to his being
appointed private secretary to the Prince of
Cobourg. " Your recent appointments I hope are
a step to something still better. In my opinion,
the service of a court can hardly be too well paid,
for immense must be the sacrifice of time and
feeling required for it." She continues : " You
are very kind in your hints as to the sort of
composition which might recommend me at
present, and I am fully sensible that an historical
romance, founded on the House of Saxe Cobourg,
might be much more to the purpose of profit or
popularity than such pictures of domestic life
in country villages as I deal in. But I could no
more write a romance than an epic poem. I
could not sit seriously down to write a serious
romance under any other motive than to save
my life, and if it were indispensable for me to
keep it up and never relax into laughing at
myself or at other people, I am sure I should be
hung before I had finished the first chapter.
No, I must keep to my own style and go on in
my own way ; and though I may never succeed
again in that, I am convinced that I should
totally fail in any other."

After this, the Reverend James Stanier Clarke

vanishes from the scene, probably a little chagrined at the rebuffs given to his suggestions, and perhaps a little suspicious that Miss Austen had not been quite so impressed by his person and his position as he had anticipated.

The number of the *Quarterly Review* which appeared in March 1816 contained a criticism of Jane's work. Writing to John Murray, she says : " The Authoress of *Emma* has no reason, I think, to complain of her treatment in it, except in the total omission of *Mansfield Park*. I cannot but be sorry that so clever a man as the Reviewer of *Emma* should consider it as unworthy of being noticed." The clever man alluded to was Walter Scott. The review is not unkindly, but is without enthusiasm. He says : " The faults of these works arise from the minute detail which the author's plan comprehends. Characters of folly or simplicity, such as those of old Woodhouse and Miss Bates, are ridiculous when first presented, but if too often brought forward, or too long dwelt on, their posing is apt to become as tiresome in fiction as in real society." This is certainly in contradiction to what Scott wrote in his *Diary* ten years later, where he says : " Read again for the third time at least Miss Austen's finely written novel of *Pride and Prejudice*. This young lady has a talent for describing the involvements and feelings and characters of modern life, which is to me the most wonderful I ever met with. The big Bow-wow strain I can do myself like any now going, but the exquisite touch which renders ordinary commonplace things and characters interesting from the truth of the description and the sentiment is denied me. What a pity such a gifted creature died so early ! "

Jane would be gratified by the fact of at last receiving attention from a literary review, but it is likely that she was more influenced by the comments of relations and friends, of which she made notes. Thus we learn that Mr. and Mrs. James Austen did not like *Emma* " as well as either of the others." Mrs. Austen found it more entertaining but not so interesting. Mrs. Digweed says, " If she had not known the author would hardly have got through it." In contrast to Mr. Jeffrey (of the *Edinburgh Review*), who was " kept up by it three nights."

It is curious that Jane's work had little real acclaim in her lifetime. This may well have been a disappointment to her, though she underestimated its value, and probably she would have been astonished, and even a little perturbed, had she anticipated the praise which has been given to her writings during the past century, and upon how solid a basis her fame now rests. She would

have been more gratified if she could have anticipated the affection with which her novels are
held. The fact that her works continue to give
the liveliest pleasure and amusement to modern
readers – and many will echo Sir John Squire's
dictum : " Nobody who likes Jane Austen can be
wholly bad or wholly stupid " – would have delighted her more than the encomiums of a hundred critics, or the fact that Macaulay likened her
work to Shakespeare. Tennyson did likewise,
saying : " The realism and life-likeness of Miss
Austen's *dramatis personæ* come nearest to those
of Shakespeare." But she would have been more
pleased – one can indeed imagine her giving a
little shiver of satisfaction, a sudden lowering and
then a swift raising of her eyebrows – had she been
told the notorious story that, when the Poet
Laureate visited Lyme Regis, and friends wished
to show him the place where Monmouth landed,
he exclaimed impatiently : " Don't talk to me of
the Duke of Monmouth. Show me the exact spot
where Louisa Musgrove fell ! "

CHAPTER V

1816–1817

In the spring of 1816 the Austens were greatly perturbed when the banking house of Austen, Maunde & Tilson, of which Henry was a partner, was compelled to close, and Henry declared bankrupt. The chief cause of the failure was the insolvency of a branch of the bank at Alton, for which the London firm had pledged itself. Henry was acquitted of any charge of personal extravagance, and it was proved that he had behaved honourably, but the whole matter was a shock to the Austens. And a financial loss to more than one member of the family. Jane herself modestly lost the sum of £13.

It was about this time that her health first showed signs of failing. She appears to have lost something of her vivacity, and to have indulged in a melancholy foreign to her character. This mood, however, was not constant. During the summer she exerted herself as usual to amuse, in her own charming and individual manner, her nephews and nieces, one of whom writes of Jane

turning out her wardrobe to provide clothes for
dressing-up, and, once, of " giving a conversation
as between myself and my two cousins, the day
after a ball." Still she played the piano for them,
gave her little exhibitions of mimicry, told stories,
and, if it were needed, provided guidance.

She had a deep affection for these young people,
but most of all for Fanny Knight, for whom she
had grieved so greatly on the death of the child's
mother. " You are inimitable, irresistable. You
are the delight of my Life. Such Letters, such
entertaining Letters as you have lately sent !
Such a description of your queer little heart !
Such a lovely display of what your Imagination
does. – You are worth your weight in Gold, or
even in the new Silver Coinage. – You are the
Paragon of all that is Silly & Sensible, commonplace and eccentric. . . . Oh ! what a loss it
will be when you are married. You are too
agreeable in your single state, too agreeable as a
Niece. I shall hate you when your delicious play
of Mind is all settled down into conjugal &
maternal affections. . . . And yet I do wish you
to marry very much, because I know you will
never be happy till you are ; but the loss of a
Fanny Knight will never be made up to me. . . ."

But that was written in the following year, a
few months before Jane's death, when Fanny was

IA

seeking her advice concerning a certain Mr. Wildman, who was eager to marry her. There is in her words a hint of hysteria, a suggestion that she was clinging almost desperately to the affection of the young, delicious Fanny, half jealous that her love might be given elsewhere, yet desperately eager for her happiness. They are an echo of that sense of fear and farewell which her friends the Fowles had remarked when, on her last visit to them at Kintbury, they noticed " she went about her old haunts, and recalled old re-collections connected with them in a particular manner, as if she did not ever expect to see them again."

The nature of the slowly progressive malady from which Jane suffered is not easy to diagnose. She speaks of pains in her back, of rheumatism, of being less and less able to take exercise, or make any exertion. In those days it would have been called a " decline," but the term is not fully illuminating ; and it is likely that Jane was con-sumptive, though there appears to have been no hereditary taint among the Austens. They were a long-lived family ; only the mysterious George seems to have been an invalid, and he lived to be over sixty.

Some time during 1816, Henry bought back the manuscript of *Northanger Abbey* from the publisher

who had purchased it in 1803, giving him the
sum of £10 which he had originally paid, and,
only when the transaction was complete, in-
formed him that it was a work by the authoress
of *Pride and Prejudice*. By August, Jane had
finished *Persuasion*, but not to her liking. For
once she was not wholly satisfied with her work,
and, after some indecision, took out the penulti-
mate chapter and wrote two chapters in its place.
But when this was done, she made no effort to
arrange that the novel should be published. She
kept it beside her, probably making minor re-
visions, and even when, in March 1817, she tells
Fanny Knight that she has something ready for
publication, she mentions that it " may perhaps
appear about a twelvemonth hence." A delay for
which there appears no reason unless she was still
unsatisfied with her work, and in particular with
the character of Anne Elliot, for she declares to
Fanny : " You may *perhaps* like the Heroine, as
she is almost too good for me."

At some period in 1816, Jane amused herself
by drawing up the outline of a novel " according
to hints from various quarters." It is in the nature
of a *jeu d'esprit*. Among the notes are the following : " The scene will be for ever shifting from
one set of people to another. The wicked will be
completely depraved and infamous, hardly a

resemblance of humanity left to them. . . .
Wherever the heroine goes somebody falls in love
with her. She is often carried away by the anti-
hero, but rescued either by her father or the hero.
Often reduced to support herself and her father
by her talents ; continually cheated ; worn to a
skeleton, and now and then starved to death."

One imagines that Jane verbally embroidered
this tale with all manner of absurdities for the
amusement of herself and of Cassandra, inventing
the most preposterous of adventures for her
heroine, exaggerating the honour and nobility of
her hero, and smirching, without compunction,
the character of her villain.

Throughout the year Jane's health continued
to cause anxiety to her family, and it was decided
she should take a course of the waters at Chelten-
ham. The visit was paid, but the result proved
disappointing, and she returned to Chawton little
benefited. There the autumn and early winter
passed quietly. Few letters of this time survive.
There is one to her nephew, James Edward
Austen, full of her accustomed humour and
raillery, one to Anna Lefroy, in which she says :
" Your Grandmother is *very* much obliged to you
for the Turkey, but cannot help grieving that you
should not keep it for yourselves. Such High-
mindedness is almost more than she can bear,"

and a note to her niece, Cassandra Austen, wish-
ing her a happy New Year, which is written
backwards, so that its ending reads, " Ruoy
Etanoitceffa Tnua." In these letters there are no
references to her state of health, but there seems
to have been a fleeting improvement, for, writing
to a friend in January 1817, she says : " I have
certainly gained strength through the winter and
am not far from being well ; and I think I understand my own case now so much better than I did,
as to be able by care to keep off any serious return
of illness. I am more & more convinced that
bile is at the bottom of all I have suffered, which
makes it easy to know how to treat myself." And
in another letter : " I feel myself getting stronger
than I was half a year ago, & can so perfectly
well walk to Alton, *or* back again, without the
slightest fatigue that I hope to be able to do both
when Summer comes." Nevertheless, she was
living the life of an invalid, with a patience and
fortitude which is manifest by the fact that she
made a couch for herself by placing two chairs together, so that Mrs. Austen should be able to lie
on the single sofa at Chawton Cottage, to which
she was accustomed.

Her spirit was strong, however, and at the end
of January she began a new novel, to which the
name of *Sanditon* has been given. The story

begins admirably : " A Gentleman & Lady travelling from Tunbridge towards that part of the
Sussex Coast which lies between Hastings and E.
Bourne, being induced by Business to quit the
high road, & attempt a very rough Lane, were
overturned in toiling up its long ascent, half rock,
half sand." The principal characters are a Lady
Denham and a Mr. Parker ; the latter enthusiastic that Sanditon should become a popular
watering-place. His enthusiasm is to some degree
shared by Lady Denham, but with reservations.
She disliked, for instance, the idea of a doctor
coming to the place, and declared : " We go on
very well as we are. There is the Sea & the
Downs & my Milch-asses. Here have I lived 70
good years in the world & never took Physic
above twice : and never saw the face of a Doctor
in all my Life on my own account." Other
characters are Mr. Parker's two sisters, and a Miss
Charlotte Heywood, a nervous and subservient
woman, who is their guest.

There is no hint how the story would have
developed, but the fragment is written in a vein
of high comedy, and the sentimental interests are
less marked than usual in Jane's work. The
characterisation is as deft and humorous as ever,
the whole has spirit and attack, and there are few
signs of any diminution of her powers in the

twelve short chapters which she wrote in little
more than six weeks. Then the power flagged.
On 17th March, the manuscript – some pages of
which were written in pencil – was abandoned.
Her malady had returned. " I certainly have
not been well for many weeks, and about a week
ago I was very poorly, I have had a good deal of
fever at times & indifferent nights, but am considerably better now, & recovering my Looks a
little, which have been bad enough, black &
white & every wrong colour. I must not depend
upon being ever very blooming again. Sickness
is a dangerous Indulgence at my time of Life."

Her health fluctuated. On a mild spring day
she goes for a drive in a donkey-cart, but a week
later she is in her room again being " coddled."
Throughout her illness she speaks of the love and
concern of her family, and again and again of the
care and attention of Cassandra. Possibly both
realised that Jane's illness was mortal, probably
each knew what the other feared, but one imagines
they never discussed what the end of these months
of dragging sickness might bring. It is likely
that Jane suffered deeply from the thought that
" dear Cassy " would be left solitary, realising
what her loss would be, and aware that even her
faith and fortitude might have faltered had it
been she who was to be left. But one imagines

that Cassandra, unflinching in her devotion, masking her own fears, was always tender and courageous, and hid her dismay at the possibility that soon the precious cord of their love and understanding might be snapped. For with Jane's death the one vital thing in her life would be destroyed. It would be dreary and colourless, and she must exist on her memories of that perfect companionship, while age crept upon her, and she became, as described by her great-niece, " a pale, dark-eyed old lady, with a high arched nose and a kind smile, dressed in a long cloak, and a large drawn bonnet, both made of black satin."

Towards the end of May, Jane writes of another " attack of my sad complaint," and for the first time there is mention of the plan of going to Winchester to be under the care of Mr. Lyford, a doctor who had already been called to Chawton after the Alton apothecary had declared that he could do no more for Miss Austen. It had been suggested that Jane should go to London, but in view of the fact that Winchester was considerably nearer, and that Mr. Lyford had already proved that he understood the case, this plan was abandoned. Jane writes almost cheerfully of the prospect, and there are touches of her familiar humour in the letter. But it ends on a note of

seriousness. " I have not mentioned my dear
Mother ; she suffered much for me when I was
at the worst but is tolerably well. – Miss Lloyd
too has been all kindness. In short, if I live to be
an old Woman, I must expect to wish I had died
now ; blessed in the tenderness of such a Family,
& before I had survived either them or their
affection. – But the Providence of God has
restored me – & may I be more fit to appear
before him when I *am* summoned, than I sh^d
have been now ! "

The journey to Winchester was made towards
the end of May. Jane drove in a carriage lent by
her brother James. Henry Knight and his son,
William, rode beside the carriage, and Jane was
distressed because rain fell most of the time, and
they got a wetting. She stood the fatigue of the
journey tolerably well, and speaks with content
of the lodgings which they had engaged. These
were in College Street. The house is still standing, and it is not difficult to imagine the two
sisters at the bow-window of the sitting-room on
the second floor, which in their day overlooked
the garden of a Dr. Gabell. Beyond was the
wall of the Close, and the grey towers of the
Cathedral.

At first Jane's strength was maintained. " My
attendant is encouraging," she writes, " and talks

of making me quite well. I live chiefly on the sofa, but am allowed to walk from one room to the other. I have been out once in a sedan-chair, and am to repeat it, and be promoted to a wheel-chair as the weather serves." She had friends in Winchester, one of her nephews was at the College, and both Henry and James visited her. But the respite from suffering was fleeting. In June, Mr. Lyford told the family, " her case is desperate," and that there was no hope of recovery.

For a little this decree may have been kept from her, but it is likely that Jane, with her candour and fearlessness, soon demanded the truth from her doctor, and during the following weeks had no incertitude regarding her condition, which she bore, as Henry testifies, " with more than resignation, with a truly elastic cheerfulness. She retained her faculties, her memory, her fancy, her temper, and her affections, warm, clear, and unimpaired to the last."

What were her thoughts as she lay in her room during those weeks of summer, listening idly to the footsteps of passers-by in the street below, and to the chiming of the Cathedral bells ? Was she satisfied with the life she had lived, or did she regret that she had had no opportunities of leading one fuller and more varied ? Was she content that, unlike all the young ladies of her novels,

she had failed to find the husband, which in their
eyes was so essential, not only for happiness but
for self-esteem?   And that her children were
those of her fancy alone?

One would like to know in what spirit she considered this large and articulate family. For
some, obviously she had a strong affection ; a
few she would deride, but she would despise none
of them, not even the most foolish. For, in spite
of the sharpness of her irony, she was tolerant.
Perhaps in those hot days of July, when life was
slipping from her so fast, the creatures of her
imagination would become vivid and insistent.
Almost they might appear to her, solicitous and
condoling, forgetting their sentiments and their
snobberies in respect for the suffering and weak-
ness of their creator. As she sat alone, the walls
of the little room in College Street might expand,
and, as if in a pleasant garden, Jane's dear characters would walk before her. The heroines in
their muslins and poplins ; the heroes with their
knee-breeches and their stocks, eyeing one another
discreetly. Under a shady tree, Mr. Bennett
might listen somewhat impatiently to the trepida-
tions of Mr. Woodhouse, while Sir William Elliot
paid no attention at all, absorbed in the Baronet-
age. A dozen children would play at hide-and-
seek in the shrubbery ; while in a gazebo, Lady

Catherine de Bourgh, marvellously condescending, would declare her opinions to a cluster of ladies, which included Miss Bates, Mrs. Jennings, and Mrs. Norris, their heads, under turbans and nodding plumes, bent forward in attention. Other figures would pass in the distance. Black-coated Mr. Collins, wondering which group he had best join. The two Miss Thorpes, giggling together. Even Lady Susan might be there, talking, perhaps, to Edward Ferrars. And all these people would move to the faint music of an orchestra, playing a dance tune.

Then the vision would pass. The walls of the room contract. Once more the bells of the Cathedral chimed, and, as the echoes faded, Jane would long for the return of Cassandra, who had gone into the town upon some errand, or hope that Henry might come ; and then, as the minutes passed, she would indulge in memories. She would think of her youth, now so distant, when her zest for life was ardent, and her future less easily anticipated than that of Elizabeth Bennett or Catherine Morland. Perhaps she had been vain and foolish, but why not ? Life, really, was not so solemn a business. Not then, at all events. Indeed, she doubted if it should ever be so – even now, when she was ill, and those whom she loved so grieved for her ;

when death was near.   And then she would think
of those who had died : her father, Madame
Lefroy, the gay, vivacious Elizabeth, Mr. Blackall.
. . . How strange and brief was that happiness !
How, otherwise, life might have been had it en-
dured. . . . But Jane's was not a mind for regrets.
With a sigh, caught back almost before it had
escaped her lips, deliberately turning away from
the years that were gone, she focused her thoughts
on the future. Hidden, alas ! Would Henry
continue to find fulfilment in his religion ?
Would Anna continue to write novels ? Whom
would Fanny marry ? Would her two sailor
brothers, after spending their lives half across
the world, end them in England ? Would dear
Cassandra find reconciliation in her loneliness ?
Why not ? She reminded herself once more that
life was really not so solemn a business. There
were always men and women to watch and marvel
at. The comedy went on. . . .

And then the door would open. Dear Cassandra had returned, a parcel in her hand, anxious,
loving, fearful of any change that might have
occurred in her brief absence. And Jane would
give her a reassuring smile.

The end was sudden. On the 15th of July
she was capable of writing some vivacious and
amusing verses on the subject of Winchester Races.

But this was a final, and, for those who watched, must have been a pitiful, flicker of her spirit, for, almost immediately after, she became gravely ill, and died three days later.

Cassandra describes the end in a letter she wrote to Jane's beloved niece, Fanny. The letter begins: " My dearest Fanny – doubly dear to me now for her dear sake whom we have lost . . . such a treasure, such a sister, such a friend as never can have been surpassed – she was the sum of my life, the gilder of every pleasure, the soother of every sorrow, I had not a thought concealed from her, & it is as if I had lost a part of myself.   I loved her only too well, not better than she deserved, but I am conscious that my affection for her made me sometimes unjust to & negligent of others, & I can acknowledge, more than as a general principal, the justice of the hand which has struck this blow."   And then she writes of Jane's death : " She felt herself to be dying about half an hour before she became tranquil and apparently unconscious.   During that half hour was her struggle, poor soul : she said she could not tell us what she suffered, tho' she complained of little fixed pain.   When I asked her if there was anything she wanted, her answer was she wanted nothing but death & some of her words were ' God grant me patience, Pray for me oh pray for me.'

Her voice was affected but as long as she spoke
she was intelligible. I hope I do not break your
heart my dearest Fanny by these particulars.
I mean to afford you gratification whilst I am
relieving my own feelings. I could not write so
to anybody else. . . . "

She goes on to describe how Jane drifted into
unconsciousness, and lay insensible, her head
propped on a pillow on Cassandra's lap, for
several hours throughout the summer night,
until, at dawn, the watchers saw that she no
longer breathed.

The funeral took place five days later, when
Jane was buried in Winchester Cathedral.
Cassandra did not attend the service, but in the
letter which she wrote to Fanny, she describes
how she watched " the little mournful procession
the length of the street," and adds : " Never
was human being more sincerely mourned by
those who attended her remains than this dear
creature."

The grave is in the north aisle of the Cathedral
In the same bay of the aisle is a memorial window,
and beneath it a brass, but the inscription upon
the plain slab of black marble which covers the
grave is nearer to her spirit and her character.
Though, maybe, she herself would have preferred
the simpler obituary, written, it seems evident,

by her brother, Henry, which appeared in *the Salisbury and Winchester Journal* of 28th July, 1817. After chronicling her death, and referring to her as the authoress of the four novels published in her lifetime, it ends : " Her manners were most gentle, her affections ardent, her candour was not to be surpassed, and she lived and died as became an humble Christian."

A SHORT BIBLIOGRAPHY

A Memoir of Jane Austen, by her nephew, J. E. Austen Leigh.   Richard Bentley & Son.   1870.

Letters of Jane Austen, edited by Edward, Lord Brabourne.   Richard Bentley & Son.   1884.

Jane Austen : Her Homes and her Friends, by Constance Hill.   John Lane.   1901.

Jane Austen's Sailor Brothers, by J. H. Hubback and Edith C. Hubback.   John Lane.   1906.

Jane Austen : Her Life and her Letters, by William Austen-Leigh and Richard A. Austen-Leigh. Smith Elder & Co.   1913.

Jane Austen (English Men of Letters) by Francis Warre Cornish.   Macmillan & Co.   1913.

Personal Aspects of Jane Austen, by Mary A. Austen-Leigh.   John Murray.   1920.

Jane Austen : A Bibliography, by Geoffrey Keynes. The Nonsuch Press.   1929.

Jane Austen's Letters, collected and edited by R. W. Chapman.   The Clarendon Press.   1932.